Our Blood and Tears:
Black Freedom Fighters

About the Book

A black named David Walker said in 1829 that "America is more our country than it is the whites'—we have enriched it with our blood and tears." Around vivid portraits of three great black leaders of their people—Benjamin Banneker, Nat Turner, and Frederick Douglass—author Ruth Wilson has woven the bitter, dramatic story of the black struggle for freedom from pre-Revolutionary days to the years following the Civil War. This is American history as blacks saw and lived it. Thus it offers new outlooks and fresh insights to peoples of all races.

Our
Blood and Tears

BLACK FREEDOM FIGHTERS

by Ruth Wilson

G. P. PUTNAM'S SONS • NEW YORK

12 up

Contents

America is more our country
than it is the whites'—we
have enriched it with our
blood and tears.

Part I

Benjamin Banneker and the Age of Reason

1

The Afro-American

One day in the year 1707, a tall black man climbed out of the hold of a ship and stumbled down the gangplank onto a wooden deck. As his eyes adjusted to the sunshine, he pulled his aching body up straight and looked around him. Behind him lay a nightmare. Before him lay—what? He had no way of knowing.

The wharf around him was crowded with white people who all seemed to be talking at once in strange, harsh sounds that made no sense at all. Closer to him, herded together in a tight little group, were his fellow passengers, Africans like himself. But even these spoke in tongues he couldn't understand as they murmured words of comfort to one another. They were a pitiable sight. The inhuman treatment of the past three months had left its mark on their bodies and in their eyes. But when their eyes fell on the tall, erect man in their midst, fear and misery gave place to an awed respect.

The black men knew instinctively what the white men would never guess. Here was a prince among men.

Not far off, a white man from the ship seemed to be having an argument with a slim young white girl. From the set of the girl's jaw, it was easy to guess who was going to win, and by the way the pair kept looking over at him, it was clear that he was involved in the heated exchange. At last the young girl came over and looked up to his face. More strange, confusing sounds—but these were accompanied by gestures, and the gestures made sense. She was asking his name.

A wave of anger and rebellion swept over the man. He wanted to strike out against this white person, against all white people who were in any way responsible for his being there, on that dock, under the hot sun. But the past months had taught him the uselessness of rebellion. He pulled himself up straighter. "Bannaky," he said proudly.

"Bannaky," she repeated.

That was the only word that passed between those two on that sunny day because neither one could speak the other's language. Yet this black man and white woman were destined to become the grandparents of the famous Benjamin Banneker.

A man from Africa and a woman from England met on a dock in the colony of Maryland. How did they get there? What had led them across the ocean to the New World?

A force as cruel and inhuman as the world had ever known had brought Bannaky from his African home, but what of the young white woman whose name was Molly Welsh? Why was she there?

The first white colonists who made the difficult ocean voyage to America did so for a variety of reasons. Some sought adventure in the new and strange continent. Others, like the Puritans and Quakers, were looking for a place where they could practice their religion free from persecution. Politics and religion played their part in the founding of the American Colonies, but the chief force behind the immigration was an economic one.

The vast majority of the settlers were ordinary people who came to America to make a better life for themselves. They were poor tenant farmers, unemployed laborers, and tradesmen who were finding it difficult to make a living in England, where there was a great deal of unemployment at the time. The vast and fertile lands of America offered a new chance to seek their fortunes. Land was there, practically for the asking, but before it could yield a profit, the work of many hands was needed to clear and cultivate it.

The English government, hoping that the rich New World would enrich the realm, was willing to support these adventurers. It chartered stock companies and appointed proprietors, giving them control over huge tracts of land. For those who were too poor to pay for the long ocean trip, a plan was worked out. In exchange for their passage, these people became indentured servants. They had to work on the land of their temporary "masters" until their period of service was up. Then they were free once more and were given some land of their own to start a new life in the New World.

In the year 1632, the fertile land north of the Potomac River and south of Pennsylvania was given by the King of England to Lord Baltimore and his heirs. At that

time no one but American Indians lived there. Lord
Baltimore named the territory Maryland and did all he
could to encourage Englishmen to settle there. Many
agreed to come, but many more were needed.

The English government was willing to supply them.
The idea of keeping convicted criminals in jails at government expense did not appeal to the men of that day.
Instead, the king ordered the worst offenders to be executed, and the rest were shipped to the Colonies of the
New World. The trip was paid for by the Britsh crown,
but when the convicts reached the Colonies, they were
obliged to work as servants for seven years before they
could have their freedom. "His Majesty's seven-year
passengers," as these people were called, were really
sentenced to seven years of hard labor in a foreign country with no hope of returning when their time was up.

Just how many people made the voyage to the Colonies in this way is not known. Among them were a wide
variety of offenders. Some were accused of nothing
worse than stealing a loaf of bread. Some were young
people who would be called juvenile delinquents today.
Others were guilty of much graver crimes.

Molly Welsh had been working as a servant on a
cattle farm in England, where part of her daily work
was to milk the cows. One day her master charged her
with stealing a pail of milk. Molly claimed that she had
not stolen the milk, that it had been spilled when a cow
kicked over the pail. But no one would take her word
against her master's. Although she was still in her teens,
she was sentenced to seven years as a servant in the
faraway colony of Maryland.

When she arrived in the New World, Molly was

assigned to a tobacco planter who had a large tract of land on the Patapsco River, about ten miles west of the small town of Baltimore. For seven years she worked on the farm as a dairy maid and part-time field hand, hoeing tobacco along with the men. It was hard work but she was learning many things about growing tobacco and corn. And in the evenings she had time to read her Bible, which she had brought with her from England—the only thing she could really call her own.

When her time of service was up and she was free, Molly Welsh moved on up the Patapsco River and settled on land of her own. She may have managed to save up money to buy a few acres. Land in the wilds of Maryland was not very expensive in those days. Or she may have just laid out her own stakes in the woods and claimed the place as "squatter's rights."

People who knew her said she was "a person of exceedingly fair complexion and moderate mental power." It is certain that she was also a person of great courage and determination.

How she managed to survive in those first months on her own it is impossible to guess. True, her land was good, with a fine spring of water on it, but it had to be cleared of brush and trees before it could be farmed. This was no work for a woman alone.

Then there were the Indians. Surely Molly must have made friends with them somehow, or she never would have survived at all. But survive she did, and soon she was making her way back down the Patapsco River to the landing wharf on Chesapeake Bay to buy two slaves who would help her farm her land. Where did she get the money? No one really knows.

One of the slaves she bought was the tall African, Bannaky.

Through the years, the story has been handed down that Bannaky was a prince. There is no reason to doubt it. It was told that he was the eldest son of a powerful African chief and that he had been kidnapped by Arab traders who sold him into slavery. His father, the chief, was furious and took revenge on the Arabs in a most brutal way. But he was powerless to get back his son. Bannaky had become one of the forty million Africans who were victims of the inhuman slave trade.

The first African slave traders were Moslems. For several centuries they dragged their black captives over the Sahara to the Middle East. Then, in 1444, the Portuguese came and established trading posts on the West Coast of Africa. Later, with the opening up of the New World by Christopher Columbus, the slave trade became big business. The fertile lands of North and South America and the West Indies offered great possibilities to planters, but labor was needed to cultivate the land— cheap labor. The African slave trade offered that cheap labor. European countries fought for monopoly of the trade. Portugal lost out to Holland. Holland lost out to France and England. And it was the English most of all who organized the cruel business.

Most of the black men who were sold into slavery came from the West Coast of Africa. They came from many different tribes. Some were captured in native wars. Some were kidnapped by Europeans or Africans. Others were sold because of their crimes against tribal laws.

Once they fell into the hands of the slavers, these

blacks were chained two by two and led to a "factory" on the seacoast. There they were branded on their chests and put into a dungeon called a Negro house to wait for a ship. To the factory the Europeans sent cloth, rum, trinkets, and other goods to be traded for these human beings.

When a shipload was ready, the slaves were rowed out to the ships, still in chains. There they were packed in spaces so small they could scarcely turn over, and under these terrible conditions they made the ten-week voyage to the New World.

Of the forty million black men and women stolen from their African homes, only about half lived through that voyage on the dreaded Middle Passage. In the crowded quarters, diseases spread quickly. Many thousands died of smallpox. Many more committed suicide or went mad. Those who survived might end up on one of the islands of the Caribbean, in Chile, Peru, or Brazil, in Mexico, or in one of the many ports of the American Colonies.

An African just off a slave ship was a dangerous man. He might be sick and half-dead from the brutal journey, but he was burning with rage against his white captives. Though his body was held in chains, his spirit was still free, and he was proud and sure of his identity as a black man. White plantation owners naturally were afraid of such a man. Before he could be of use as a slave, the African had to be taught how to be a slave. He had to go through a "breaking-in" period which usually lasted from one to three years. During this time, he was taught a kind of pidgin English. Since his fellow slaves came from many different African tribes and each spoke his own native tongue, this new language was needed if he was to talk with blacks as well as with white men. He was given a new name and was forced to look at himself and others in a new way. He was taught that he was expected to work for his master all day, every day of his life. He was taught the cruel reality of what it meant to long for freedom and to live as a slave.

There was only one way to teach a black man these things, and that was with a whip. Slave breakers whipped their slaves to the point of death in an effort to break their rebellious spirit.

Bannaky was spared this cruel breaking-in period. "Unbroken" slaves were much cheaper to buy because they were a danger to their white owners. No doubt it was lack of money that moved Molly Welsh to buy her slaves directly from the captain of a slave ship, and no doubt the captain tried to talk her out of it. But Molly Welsh was a determined young woman, so when she started back up the river to her spring and her land, Bannaky and another slave from the same ship went with her. No record exists of the other slave's name.

Molly Welsh had her hands full. She couldn't reason with the men because they didn't speak the same language. She couldn't beat them into submission because she was not as strong as they. For a while, it looked as if she had made a poor bargain. Try as she would, she could not get Bannaky to do any work. He lay in the sun, bathed in the brook, amused himself in the woods, but he would not work. Molly adopted the policy of "no work, no food." This was successful as far as the other slave was concerned, but it did not work with Bannaky. Moreover, every time she gave the worker his food, he turned around and gave it to Bannaky. Bannaky accepted it as though it were his due and went about his own business.

As the three gradually learned to speak to each other, Molly discovered the reason for this. Since Bannaky was the son of an African chief, he was considered to be above manual work. Molly had to make the best of the situation.

Though Bannaky refused to be Molly Welsh's slave, he was willing—more than willing—to be her husband. A few years later, in 1715, Maryland passed a law forbidding the marriage of any white with "any Negro or Mulatto slave," but at the time that Bannaky married Molly such marriages were quite frequent. When Molly Welsh became Molly Bannaky, she freed both of her slaves. "The other slave" must have gone off by himself. Nothing more is known of him. But Bannaky became master of the land on the upper Patapsco River. It soon became known as Bannaky's Springs and was the envy of the settlers for miles around.

The proud Bannaky refused to let anyone baptize him, so he never received a Christian name. He was always simply "Bannaky." He was described as "a man of much intelligence and fine temper, with a very agreeable presence, dignified manner and contemplative habits." For fifteen years he worked on his own farm. Using the methods he had known in Africa, he channeled the water from the spring into canals to irrigate his fields. Thus, even when other fields of tobacco were drying up from lack of rain, Bannaky's crops were good.

Four children were born to the couple, but when the

eldest was only fourteen, Bannaky, the proud black prince, died. According to the story that has been told for countless years, he was claimed by his gods. In the midst of a raging storm, he was struck by lightning. Friendly Indians carried him home and gave him a chief's burial.

Molly lived on with her children in the cabin Bannaky had built for her on the top of the hill above the spring. She never forgot her black prince, and when her eldest child, Mary, was old enough to marry, she remembered her own happiness and decided the girl should do as she had done.

Mary Bannaky was a free mulatto, a pretty girl who could have had her pick of several men, but she was content to let her mother choose her husband. So once again, Molly went down to the landing to meet one of the slave ships. She made her choice carefully and paid a good price. The new slave was given the Christian name of Robert, and after his marriage to Mary, he became known as Robert Bannaky.

All his life Robert Bannaky bore the marks of his cruel journey to America. His eyes had a fierce, haunted look, and the ankle chains he had been forced to wear had scarred and twisted his foot so that he walked with a limp. But he was big and strong. He caught on quickly to the farming methods of the first Bannaky, and under his hands the land continued to be fruitful. He built a home for his young bride on the corner of Molly's property, using as his model the African huts he had known in his native land. The six sides of the hut were made of small branches woven together. The roof was rounded and thatched. Practical for the warm climate of

Africa, the hut was not very well suited to the cold winters of Maryland.

It was here in the home so similar to those of his black forefathers that Benjamin Bannaky was born on November 9, 1731.

He was Robert and Mary's first child and Molly's first grandchild. From his birth he was his grandmother's favorite. She seemed to see in him the image of her beloved husband. She taught him all the ancient African wisdom she had learned from Bannaky, and she read to him out of the only book she owned, her Bible. With Benny to love, Molly was once more contented.

But as the years passed and his own family grew, Robert Bannaky was no longer contented. Soon three little daughters were born, and the thatched hut was much too small. His wife's younger brother, Ned, was grown now and had brought a wife to live with Molly in the cabin on the hill. Robert didn't want to work for someone else. He wanted land of his own. Molly understood this and promised to help.

At last, when Benny was six years old, the time came. The season had been a good one—the tobacco crop was one of the best. It was hard work to harvest and smoke it. Each leaf had to be picked as it ripened and then carefully cured in the smokehouse. Benny and his little sister, Minta, worked alongside their father and Uncle Ned. And when all was harvested, there were 7,000 pounds of tobacco ready for market.

Carefully, the huge golden leaves were packed into large wooden casks known as hogsheads. The top was closed tight, and a long pole was passed through the center of the cask. The hogshead became a huge wheel with the pole as its axle.

Benny and his grandmother went with the men to market. Starting at dawn, they rolled the great hogsheads through the woods along a path called the rolling road. With a man holding the pole at each end, the tobacco could be guided along the twisting road. It was slow going. Each night they made camp in the woods, and four days later they reached the market town.

Molly Bannaky, the white woman, went along with her son-in-law to make sure that justice was done. As the tobacco was weighed, she stood close at hand, and when the sale of land took place it was she who signed for her daughter's husband. Then she read out the deed for all to hear: "For seven thousand pounds of tobacco delivered this day, Richard Gist conveys one hundred and twenty acres to Robert Bannaky and Benjamin Bannaky, his son."

That was in the year 1737. Benjamin was only six years old, but he had become a landowner in the colony of Maryland.

Robert Bannaky's new land was next to Molly's Bannaky's Springs. He dug new ditches on it, and by a system of locks and gates he was able to carry the spring water through his fields. He chose the place for his new house carefully. Experience had proven that the thatched hut was not practical for America, so the new house was made of logs with a stone fireplace. It was divided into two rooms, and there were windows to let in the light. Into this fine new home he moved his little family—Mary, his mulatto wife, his daughters

different from that of most black Americans of his time. The vast majority of these were slaves, and it was as slaves that they left their mark on the country. Out of their misery and hard work, the American Colonies grew. In fact, it is doubtful that the country could have survived without the constant, oppressive labor of these unfortunate people.

By 1707, when Banneker's grandfather arrived in America, slavery was firmly established in Virginia, Maryland, and the Carolinas. With this enforced labor, Southern planters could cultivate huge tracts of land and export crops at a large profit. In New England, where farming methods were different, slaves were not used very much, but New Englanders profited from the black man by adding the slave trade to their other commerce. In the North and South alike, white men were getting rich at the expense of the men from Africa.

The work done by the slaves was so necessary to the survival and growth of the country that white men blinded themselves to the misery of their fellow human beings and tried to justify the slave system on economic grounds. They eased their consciences by claiming it was temporary.

From the very beginning there were Americans who opposed this human bondage on religious and moral grounds. Chief among these were the Quakers who never failed to speak out against this savage practice.

Free blacks as well as slaves were treated as inferior. Laws were passed to regulate their activities, and wherever they went, they were obliged to carry papers proving that they were free. And woe to anyone caught without his papers! He might find himself overpowered by a gang of white slavers who would carry him off and sell him into slavery.

Banneker had firsthand knowledge of this type of injustice. Ned Bannaky, his uncle, was a free mulatto, born of free parents. One morning he set out for Elk Ridge Landing with a load of lumber to sell, and with the business done, he walked along the water's edge talking with his companion. Suddenly he was surrounded by a band of strange white men who demanded to see his free papers. Ned had no papers with him. He and his friend did their best to fight off the men, but in the struggle Ned was knocked unconscious and dragged aboard the slavers' small boat. His friend escaped to carry the sad news back to the family.

Ned Bannaky was never seen again. Knowing his proud nature, his family guessed that he would not live long as a slave. He would keep right on fighting until his captors killed him.

For a while his wife, Ida, lived with her children in the cabin that had belonged to Molly Bannaky, but soon she became sick and died. Mary took the children to live with her, and Ben and his father built another room onto the house so they would be comfortable in their new home. Molly Bannaky's cabin stood empty in its orchard of apple trees. Molly herself was no longer present to protect her family and its interests.

Other laws discriminated against free blacks. Marriages were forbidden between blacks and whites, and people who were one-half, one-fourth, or even one-eighth black were declared by law to be "Negroes." Even blacks who owned property and were well educated were not accepted socially.

Benjamin Banneker's fine intellect and sterling qualities had won him a place of respect in his community. His neighbors regarded him as a friend and an equal. One-fourth white and three-fourths black, he was proud of his blackness, proud to be considered an African. Yet from an economic point of view, his blackness was a handicap.

The Bannaky lands had always produced excellent tobacco, but all over Maryland and Virginia farmers were growing tobacco. There was just too much being offered for sale, and the price went down steadily. The Maryland Assembly passed laws to help the situation, and as might be expected, the laws favored the rich white landowners. Public warehouses were set up where all tobacco offered for sale was to be inspected. If the crop passed inspection, it could be sold. If not, it had to be burned. As a black grower, Banneker didn't stand a chance. No matter how good his crop was, it wouldn't pass inspection. Sadly, he watched while his beautiful leaves of golden tobacco which had received so much care and hard work went up in flames.

This was a bitter blow to the young farmer. He was forced to give up growing tobacco for export. Instead, he turned to other crops which could be sold at the local market.

About this time he found another subject that took his mind off the tobacco market completely. One of his white friends gave him a watch. It was the first time-piece he had ever seen, and it fascinated him. Like most of the people in Colonial America, he used a sundial to tell time. He knew how a sundial worked, but the little watch was much more accurate and reliable.

How did it work? Banneker was determined to find out.

He searched through all the books he could find, trying to learn all he could about the laws of motion. Which one of them would unlock the mystery of the little watch? He knew that if he was ever going to find out how it worked, he would have to take it apart. But if he did, would he ever be able to put it back together again? Finally, he decided to take the risk.

Benjamin needed a quiet place to work, and his eyes turned to the cabin on the hill. He cleaned and repaired it and covered the walls with shelves for his precious books. In the center of the room, he placed a large white worktable. He was ready to begin.

Carefully he opened the watch case and studied the movement of the wheels as they ticked off the seconds. Then, one by one, he lifted the pieces out of the case and laid them on the table. The workings of the watch were no longer a mystery. Next, he set to work measuring, studying, and drawing each part. Finally, he began the difficult task of fashioning each piece on a larger scale in wood. He was making a clock.

Every moment he could spare from the farm was spent in the cabin working at his table. Month after month went by. The watch was back in its case and working well again. It had served well as a model. Still, the new clock did not meet Banneker's high standard. Each part must be exactly shaped. The hour hand must be perfectly matched with the minute hand. A mechanism must be worked out so that the clock would strike the hour.

At last, in the year 1753 it was finished and set up

in a fine wooden case. It ran perfectly and struck each hour with a mellow tone.

News of the wonderful wooden clock spread over the countryside. Some said that Benjamin Banneker had made the first clock ever constructed in America. Perhaps in New York or Boston there were other clockmakers, but surely Banneker's was the first clock to be made in Maryland, and it made him famous.

The amazing thing was that Banneker had never even seen a clock before. He had to figure the whole thing out using the only mechanical timepiece he had, a small pocket watch. Moreover, he had made the whole thing out of wood with no other tool than a pocketknife. Even so, he had produced a perfect piece of machinery, and his wooden clock became one of the wonders of the day. Banneker was recognized as a mechanical genius.

People flocked to see him from Baltimore, Fredericktown, and Annapolis, and even from Philadelphia and New York. They came to see the remarkable clock and to hear it chime, but they stayed to talk with the amazing black inventor.

By the time Robert Bannaky died in 1756, his beloved son, Benjamin, now a young man of twenty-five, was the most honored man in the whole county.

Benjamin Banneker never married. By nature he was a loner. At the cabin on the hill he could plan his time as he chose, and often he studied all night long, going to bed for a few hours after the sun rose. After the death of his father, he took his place as the head of the family. His sisters Minta and Tillie were both married. Proud of their African heritage, both had chosen black men.

Now that he was famous as the maker of the wooden clock, Banneker was very much in demand as the mender of clocks and watches. He moved in an ever-widening circle, mending and remaking timepieces, building sundials, and solving problems of all sorts. His knowledge of engineering, natural sciences, and mathematics grew by leaps and bounds. He was so eager to read the latest journals from England that he often went down the river to Baltimore to meet the ships when they arrived.

The town of Baltimore was growing fast and promised to become an important shipping port. The Maryland government was eager to develop the area, so in 1769 a law was passed giving twenty acres of land on either side of any stream to anyone who would build a mill on it. This offer attracted the Ellicott family of Pennsylvania.

The three brothers, Joseph, John, and Andrew Ellicott, had great plans. Joseph had spent several years in Europe and had seen the small-farm system that was developing there. Why couldn't something like that work in America? Years of planting tobacco had already ruined much of the land, but large areas in western Maryland were fine for wheat. The Ellicotts planned to get farmers to grow wheat. For their part, they would build a mill to grind the wheat into flour.

They chose their site carefully, and in May, 1772, they settled near Elk Ridge Landing. With them they brought all their supplies—wagons, carts, wheelbarrows, and tools of all sorts. Soon they were joined by their wives and families and by workmen who wanted to join this exciting new experiment.

It was not long before the Ellicotts heard of the remarkable black man who lived in the area. Benjamin
Banneker was exactly the man they needed to help them
set up the mill. Banneker was willing, and so a friend-
ship was started which would last for many years. The
Ellicotts were Quakers and entirely free from race
prejudice. They saw Banneker for what he was—a fine
and gifted man, proud to be black.

Banneker's mechanical ability was needed at the
new mill. He put together the machinery that had
been carried up the river in parts and pieces. For the
first time in his life, he had proper tools to work with—
chisels, planes, a compass, instruments for accurate
measurement. Soon the great wheel was turning and
the mill was ready to grind wheat into flour.

The Ellicotts were offering jobs to anyone who
wanted to work, and they offered fair prices for all
the wheat anyone could grow. By 1774 a small village
called Ellicott Mills had grown up, and Benjamin
Banneker had shown his talent in another field. Working with one of the Ellicotts, he carefully surveyed the
land and laid out the town, with straight roads running along the river and up the hill from the bank.
This knowledge of surveying was to prove important
in his later life.

Two of the Ellicotts were particularly fond of the
black man. One was George, the son of John Ellicott,
who was only sixteen when he first met Banneker. He
was greatly impressed by the tall, quiet black man,
and in spite of the difference in their ages, the two
became good friends. George was a frequent visitor to

the cabin on the hill, and often the two men talked until dawn.

Joseph Ellicott was a scientist and had a large library which he shared with his friend. He and Banneker shared other interests too, particularly their concern for the slaves.

For those who saw slavery for the great evil it was, three problems had to be faced: how to stop the slave trade, how to abolish slavery itself, and what should be done with the slaves once they were free. Ellicott and Banneker spent long hours discussing these problems, but there were no easy solutions.

As time went on, more and more Americans agreed that the slave trade must be stopped. Many were prompted by deep concern for the welfare and rights of their fellow human beings; others had other reasons. Almost one-fifth of America's total population was made up of slaves, and no more were needed at that time. So it was for a mixture of motives that the Colonial governments began to pass laws prohibiting further importation. Virginia, North Carolina, and Georgia, as well as most of the Northern colonies, had taken this step by the year 1774.

This was a cause for rejoicing among those sincere men who really had the good of the black men at heart, but they were far from satisfied. Many worked tirelessly for abolition.

Banneker found encouragement in these signs of a better future for his brothers, but the slave issue was not the only one that dominated the news in 1774. The rising conflict between the American colonists and the British government had already led to bloodshed.

2

Revolution

The end of the French and Indian War in 1763 marked the beginning of trouble between the American colonists and the British. England's war with France for the possession of the rich lands west of the Alleghany mountains had been a costly one, and when the French were finally driven out of America, the British government was deep in debt. Since the colonists were the ones to benefit from the victory, the government claimed they should be the ones to pay the public debt. Therefore, a series of laws was passed tightening the government's control over the Colonies.

For two generations the Americans had been managing their own affairs; now the rulers in faraway England began to place restrictions on them. They were forced to pay taxes on sugar, tea, and other luxuries, and a new law was passed prohibiting the local governments from issuing paper money for the payment of debt. Worse still, a standing army of British soldiers was sent to the Colonies to be housed and fed at the colonists' expense.

With each new regulation, the discontent of the people grew. In 1765, when the Stamp Act was passed placing a tax on newspapers and legal documents, the colonists were indignant.

A wave of protest swept over the land. Newspapers were published, meetings were called, riotous demonstrations were held.

On his peaceful hill near Elk Ridge, Maryland, Benjamin Banneker heard news of these events. Sometimes the news was weeks old by the time it reached him, since all forms of communication were slow in those days.

Far to the north, the citizens of Boston, enraged by the high taxes placed on goods shipped to that port, had organized a boycott against all British imports. In answer to this, the British sent two regiments of troops to be stationed in the center of town to protect the customs officials.

To the people of Boston, the soldiers were trespassers sent by an unfair government to enforce unfair laws, and they showed their resentment by jeers and angry remarks. For seventeen months trouble had been brewing between the soldiers and the citizens.

Among the people of Boston was a man who could not claim to be a "citizen." He was a runaway slave named Crispus Attucks. Twenty years earlier, when he had escaped from his master in Framingham, Massachusetts, the angry slaveowner put out a notice for his return, describing him as "a mulatto fellow, about 27 years of age, named Crispus, 6 feet 2 inches high, short curly hair, his knees nearer together than common."

Now he was forty-seven years old. He had learned a lot in his twenty years of freedom as he drifted from place to place. The rebellious talk of the people of Boston struck a responding chord in his heart. He too loved freedom and hated oppression.

One cold evening in March, 1770, while he was at supper near Dock Square, he heard the fire bell ring. This was the signal of alarm, and Attucks went out to see what was the matter. The center of the trouble was some distance away on King Street. There a group of citizens had attacked a soldier on sentry duty with snowballs. The frightened soldier called for help and was quickly joined by an officer and eight other soldiers who came running up with their muskets ready.

In Dock Square, about thirty excited men had gathered. Quickly, Attucks took the lead. A tall, brawny man, "whose very look was enough to terrify any person," he was a well-known figure on the Boston docks, and when he spoke, men listened. Arming the men with sticks and clubs, he led them through the streets to King Street.

As is always the case when an angry mob takes action, no one knew exactly what happened next. One of the soldiers was hit with a club. Some said it was Attucks who struck the blow; others said he was standing quietly, leaning on his stick at the time. One thing is clear—he was at the very front of the crowd confronting the soldiers when these frightened men fired their muskets. Eleven people were hit. Crispus Attucks, "the first to defy," was the first to die.

In all only five men were killed in this "Battle of King Street" on March 5, 1770, but the incident became

famous throughout the Colonies as the Boston Massacre. Three days later, the five "martyrs," one black
and four white, were carried in funeral procession
through the streets of Boston and buried in a common
grave.

Rebellion spread throughout the Colonies. Men everywhere took sides, and many supported the cause of
Massachusetts against the British government. In September, 1774, the First Continental Congress met in
Philadelphia with representatives from every colony
except Georgia. A Declaration of Rights and Grievances
was drawn up demanding that the British stop their
oppression.

A new spirit was stirring in the hearts of men. The
beginning of the eighteenth century had ushered in a
new philosophy. In the past, all questions were resolved through faith; now men undertook to solve all
problems by the use of reason. From this new point
of view, men began to ask themselves questions about
their political institutions. What was the nature of the
power these institutions possessed? Where did the power
come from? Which rights belonged to the state and
which to the individual citizen?

Thoughtful men of the day answered these questions
by defining the rights of man. Man had always possessed certain natural rights—to life, liberty, and the
pursuit of happiness. When groups of men voluntarily
banded together and set up leaders to govern them,
a social contract was established between the two
groups. The power that the leaders exercised was given
to them by the people they governed, and if the leaders
broke their contract, the people had the right to dis-

solve the government and establish one that would fulfill its obligations. If the government did not protect the rights of the men it governed, then those men were justified in revolting against it.

Many of the American colonists applied this philosophy to their own situation. The British government, by passing unjust laws, had violated the rights of the colonists. The terms of the social contract had been broken, and the need for revolution was clear.

Everywhere men were speaking of freedom. Black men, both slave and free, asked themselves the all-important question, "Freedom for whom?" The same white people who opposed British oppression were keeping the black men in cruel subjection.

Many white men were quick to see the basic conflict between the revolutionary philosophy of the rights of man and the realities of American life. Previously, slavery was opposed on moral and religious grounds. Now men stated clearly that to be free was the natural and inalienable right of every man and that the slave system violated that right.

Democratic patriots called attention to this fact. Those who opposed slavery grew in numbers, and some slaveowners freed their slaves.

Meanwhile, in the towns of Massachusetts men were drilling on the commons, forming into units of minutemen, preparing themselves to take up arms if necessary. Black and white men stood together in the ranks.

More than any others, black Americans knew the value of freedom. They were quick to catch the revolutionary spirit and welcomed the chance to take up arms.

Their chance came in the spring of 1775. The Colonial minutemen had stored arms and ammunition in the town of Concord, ready for use against the British. Early in April the rumor spread from town to town that the government forces under General Gage were planning to march on Concord and seize this small arsenal. As the British made their plans, their every move was known to the patriots.

On April 18, when the British general finally dispatched 700 soldiers to Concord, news of the troop's movements quickly spread over the countryside. The minutemen assembled for action. As the Redcoats reached the town of Lexington on the way to Concord, they were confronted by a defiant band of patriots. Seventy half-trained, poorly equipped men—tradesmen, farmers, old men, and boys in their teens—stood up against the well-trained British forces. The British opened fire and charged. Within minutes eight Americans lay dead and several more were wounded. The Battle of Lexington was over and the Revolutionary War had begun.

One of the casualties in this famous battle was a black man, Prince Estabrook, a slave from West Lexington. Pomp Blackman and Lemuel Haynes were among those who escaped British bullets and went on to fight again.

The British troops pushed on to Concord only to find that the arms they were seeking had been removed from the town. By this time, about 400 minutemen had gathered in the surrounding hills. They came from all the neighboring towns, and in their ranks several black faces were to be found. Peter Salem, who had been given his freedom so he could enlist, served with the Framingham company. From Cambridge came Cato Stedman and Cato Bordman; Cuff Whittemore and Cato Wood were in the Arlington forces. Pompey and "Joshua Boylston's Prince" joined ranks from Braintree and Brookline. Free man and slave, they fought for the cause of liberty.

From their positions behind trees and stone fences, they opened fire on the Redcoats. When the British turned to flee, the minutemen followed through the woods, shooting at the column of soldiers as it marched down the road on the way back to Boston.

In Boston, the British forces moved again to prevent the patriots from developing a position of strength. On June 17, under cover of heavy fire from the fleet, the British crossed the river to Charlestown and marched up Breed's Hill, where the patriots awaited them.

Among the American troops was Barzillai Lew, a black man and a veteran of the French and Indian War. During lulls in the fighting of what became known as the Battle of Bunker Hill, he played his fife for the soldiers. Other black patriots who fought in that famous battle were Cato Tufts, Prince Hall, Cuff Hayes, Pomp Fisk, Caesar Dickerson, Sampson Talbot, Grant Cooper, Titus Coburn, and Seymour Burr. Side by side with their white comrades, these men waited as the Redcoats poured up the hill in their third attack

Cuff Whittemore, a black veteran of Lexington and Concord, received a bullet through his hat but "fought to the last." He picked up a British officer's sword that was lying on the hill and kept it as a trophy. Another black man, Caesar Brown, was less fortunate. He was one of the American casualties of the day.

With their ammunition gone, a handful of Americans fought off the British to the last man, using their guns as clubs and holding back the advance while the rest of the Americans escaped. The British won possession of Bunker and Breed's hills, but they had lost over 1,000 men. The Americans, who had lost only 500, claimed the victory.

One of the outstanding heroes at Bunker Hill was Salem Poor. This ex-slave so greatly impressed his fellow soldiers that they petitioned the Continental Congress in his behalf, stating that "the Negro called Salem Poor behaved like an experienced officer as well as an excellent soldier. . . . We only beg leave to say that in the person of this said Negro centers a brave and gallant soldier. The reward due to so great and distinguished a character, we submit to Congress."

A few weeks later, Lemuel Haynes, a veteran of the Battle of Lexington, was seeing action again at Fort Ticonderoga. Epheram Blackman and Primus Black were also there, integrating Ethan Allen's Green Mountain Boys as they captured the fort in a surprise attack. Captured also were precious supplies and ammunition which were desperately needed by the American army that began to gather outside Boston under the command of George Washington.

Now, in all the colonies men were going off to enlist in the new Continental Army. Benjamin Banneker was in his forty-fourth year, too old to fight. But he began talking to his nephews and the other young men in Maryland's Elk Ridge district, urging them to join up.

Among the young men who went down to Baltimore
to enlist was Bill Black, the son of Banneker's sister
Tillie. Bill was eighteen and an intelligent young man,
but he came back sadly. The Army had rejected him
because he was black.

What had happened? Black men had been fighting
and dying in the battles in the North. Why were they
now being turned away?

As early as May, 1775, the Committee of Safety of
Massachusetts had resolved that no slave should be
admitted into its Army, but the right of free blacks to
bear arms was not disputed. Many slaves were given
their freedom so that they could enlist, and they took
their places in the ranks with the white men. In Connecticut, Rhode Island, and New Hampshire companies,
there were "some hundreds of blacks—slaves and freemen" alike. It was definitely an integrated Army that
Washington took command of in the late summer of
1775.

However, there were many whites who were afraid
to put a gun in the hands of a slave. They claimed that
a slave with a gun was an open invitation to trouble
for themselves. Furthermore, they did not like to de-
prive the slaveowners of their slaves' services, and they
had no intention of letting the Army become a refuge
for runaway slaves.

The new federal Army could afford to be more selec-
tive than the local militias. "Many Northern blacks were
excellent soldiers," one writer remarked, "but Southern
troops would not brook an equality with the whites."
General Horatio Gates, Washington's adjutant general,
began a movement to exclude all blacks from active

service. At a meeting attended by Washington in October, 1775, Massachusetts, Rhode Island, and Connecticut reached a decision. All blacks, both slave and
free, were to be rejected. A few weeks later the Continental Congress upheld this decision.

Lord Dunmore, the royal governor of Virginia, was
loyal to the British crown and had no intention of
joining forces with the rebels. When Virginia joined
the other colonies in the fight against British oppression, he fled the colony and took up his position on a
ship anchored in the bay. From there, in November,
1775, he issued a proclamation inviting all slaves to
leave their masters and join the royal forces. The reward
for their services would be their freedom.

Moved by the same love of liberty that caused the
colonists to take up arms against the British, hundreds
of slaves flocked to answer Dunmore's call.

Since the royal forces had no base on the mainland,
the slaves joined Dunmore on his ships in Chesapeake
Bay. There they were enlisted into the military forces,
trained, and armed. Shortly after, they took part in the
skirmish at Kemp's Landing, where the Colonial forces
were routed. Later, at the Battle of Great Bridge, nearly
half of the British troops of 600 men were black. This
was Dunmore's first and only major military engage-
ment, and it was lost to the colonists. After that the
troops were completely waterbound, and the blacks were
used as seamen and pilots on the ships.

In all not more than 800 blacks succeeded in joining
Dunmore, but his proclamation quickened the desire
for freedom in the hearts of countless more. Thousands
of slaves ran away from their American masters to find

refuge and the promised freedom behind the British
lines. Many more were captured by the Redcoats in
the fighting. The British put them to good use. As
military laborers they played an important part in every
major battle until the end of the war. And when the
British troops left the country after the war, an estimated 17,000 blacks went with them, some to Canada,
some to West Africa, but most of all to the British West
Indies.

General Washington saw at once how dangerous Dunmore's proclamation was to his own cause. He changed
his policy concerning blacks as soldiers, and his alarm
was so great that he acted even before Congress gave
its approval.

In January, 1776, Congress decided that "the free
Negroes who have served faithfully in the army may be
re-enlisted therein, but no others."

Meanwhile, Washington had a war to fight. The
British were entrenched in Boston, and men came from
all over New England to join the Continental Army in
laying siege to the town. Among the New Hampshire
troops were several slaves, "effective able-bodied men,
enlisted with the consent of their masters." Blacks
served in several Connecticut companies, too, and General John Thomas, who commanded the American right
wing, wrote, "In the regiments at Roxbury we have
some Negroes, but I look on them, in general, equally
serviceable with other men, for fatigue and in action;
many of them have proved themselves brave." Law or
no law, the blacks were there.

Toward the end of 1776 the final defeat of the
American Army seemed near at hand. It consisted of

only 2,000 men, poorly clothed, badly equipped, and underfed. In spite of efforts to enlist new troops, few citizens cared to join an army that had been so badly beaten. Any able-bodied man was welcome, regardless of his color.

The turning point came on Christmas Eve. Through a blinding snowstorm, Washington led his troops across the Delaware River. With him on that fateful night were two black men, Prince Whipple and Oliver Cromwell. Whipple was in the general's own boat as it made its way through the icy waters. The British, encamped in Trenton, were taken completely by surprise. Trenton was captured, and with it a force of about 1,000 Redcoats. On went the newly victorious army to capture Princeton and draw the British back toward New York.

The next year, 1777, saw a complete change in the new nation's attitude toward black enlistment. The need for soldiers was becoming desperate. When the Continental Congress fixed troop quotas on each of the states requiring them to furnish a certain number of men, the use of black men gained support. Hundreds of slaves took up arms in the fight for freedom with their own freedom a reward for their services. Many went along with their masters as orderlies and aids. Others were enlisted as substitutes for white men who did not want to fight. No doubt it was true that a slave, accustomed to fatigue, hardened and disciplined by slavery, often made a better soldier than his master. Blacks made the best of inferior materials and short supplies and were cheerful under difficulties.

Only the Southern states continued to exclude slaves.

The many blacks who entered the ranks from Virginia were all free men.

The typical black soldier was a private in the infantry. One of these, Jack Sisson, took part in the daring capture of British General Richard Prescott, July, 1777, in Newport, Rhode Island. Sisson steered the boat as forty volunteers sailed quietly through water patrolled by the British and into the enemy camp. The general was taken by surprise and hurried off half dressed. According to one story, Sisson broke down the door of Prescott's room by butting his head against it.

Blacks were present later that year when Washington was defeated in the Battle of Brandywine. Edward Hector, one of the few to serve in the artillery, proved his bravery that day. When the order came to abandon the wagons and retreat, Hector stood his ground. Taking up the arms left on the field by the fleeing soldiers, he managed to bring his horses and ammunition wagons to safety.

Many of the blacks served as drummers. Jabez Jolly and William Nickens were two whose names are known. The Nickens family gave nine men, brothers and cousins, to the Army.

At Saratoga, when General John Burgoyne surrendered his army, still over 5,000 strong, to General Gates and his American troops, blacks were there, sharing the victory with the general who had so recently worked for their exclusion.

In victory, in defeat, in hardship, blacks were there. When Washington took up quarters at Valley Forge in the winter of 1777, blacks as well as whites suffered

the cold and privation. Without enough food or clothing, living in huts built by their own hands, many died
of starvation and cold. Others survived to be trained by
Baron von Steuben, who taught them how to work
together as a disciplined army without losing speed
and flexibility. Salem Poor, a black hero of Bunker
Hill, was one of these.

Most of the fighting forces were integrated, but there
were several all-black companies. Massachusetts and
Rhode Island each had two and Connecticut had one.
At first it was hard to get white officers to command
these troops, but finally Captain David Humphreys volunteered to head the Connecticut company. Under his
command the blacks fought so well that other white
officers were willing to act as their leaders. One of the
Massachusetts units, called Bucks of America, was commanded by a black man, Colonel Middleton.

Colonel Christopher Green's Rhode Island regiment
was made up of 125 blacks. Although they were all
newly enlisted, they took part in the Battle of Newport,
August 29, 1778. Knowing that the black regiment was
inexperienced, the enemy directed the assault toward
it. Through four hours of hard fighting, the soldiers
withstood three charges without giving ground. When
they were finally forced to withdraw, they did so in
the orderly manner of seasoned troops and were rewarded with high praise for their performance and
courage.

It has been estimated that of the 300,000 American
soldiers who served in the war about 5,000 were black.

Even before the war black men had been welcomed
as seamen, and many served in the Navy during the

war. Cato Carlile and Scipio Africanus were with Captain John Paul Jones in his battles against the British. Others served on the frigate *Boston,* where Cuff Freeman and Cato Austin manned the guns and Scipio Brown and Caesar Fairweather were powder boys. Black pilots were common, and several of these were commended for their service.

Other blacks acted as spies for the Americans. The most famous of these was James, the slave of William Armistead. He was a spy for Lafayette and brought him valuable information from the British camp. Lafayette saw to it that he was rewarded with his freedom and given a pension by the Virginia legislature. Saul Mathews, Antigua, and Pompey were other slaves who worked successfully as spies.

Late in 1778 the British began a new plan of battle. They decided to take the seaport bases in the South and move their forces north from there. By December they had captured and looted Savannah, Georgia, and were moving up through the Carolinas, burning plantations and kidnapping slaves as they went.

In Georgia a former slave won distinction for "bravery and fortitude in several engagements." He was Austin Dabney, who had been freed to serve as his master's substitute. Fighting in the artillery corp at the Battle of Kettle Creek early in 1779, he was wounded in the thigh.

Later in 1779 French troops under Count d'Estaing attempted to push the British out of Savannah. The French Army came by sea and included 545 blacks from the island of Santo Domingo. One of these, a boy in his teens, was Henri Christophe, who would one day be King of Haiti.

But when the French forces attacked, the British were ready for them. The French were forced to retreat, and it was only the black troops fighting in the rear guard that prevented the battle from becoming a complete disaster.

Congress, forced into action by British victories in the South, recommended to South Carolina and Georgia that they "take measures immediately for raising three thousand able-bodied Negroes." Owners of slaves were to be paid for them by the government.

Alexander Hamilton, writing to Congress from Army headquarters, said, "The contempt we have been taught to entertain for the blacks makes us fancy many things that are founded neither in reason nor experience." He recommended that slaves be enlisted, adding that "an essential part of the plan is to give them their freedom with their muskets."

Congress appointed John Laurens, who more than any other man believed in arming the slaves, to go to South Carolina "to raise two, three or four battalions of Negroes."

General Nathanael Greene, sent from Rhode Island to the South to reorganize the army there, joined his voice to that of Laurens, but the people of South Carolina rejected the proposal. Black troops were used for transport and labor battalions, but none were allowed in the armed forces.

In May, 1780, the British attacked Charleston from the land and sea, and the Americans were forced to surrender 5,500 men in the worst disaster of the war.

In the spring of 1781, a British army under Charles Cornwallis moved into Virginia and finally encamped at Yorktown. Chesapeake Bay became the central theater of war. And then another enemy struck the area. Yellow fever broke out in Baltimore. The disease spread quickly, causing many deaths. The epidemic reached Elk Ridge, and soon Benjamin Banneker's mother, Mary, and his sister Tillie were both dead. Banneker's old friend Joseph Ellicott was also among the victims.

Facing the British forces at Yorktown was a ragged army led by Lafayette. In it were 500 Marylanders, many free blacks who had been permitted to enlist by a decree passed in May, 1781. Maryland was still willing to take only a limited number of slaves as soldiers and refused to make them into a separate unit.

As they waited through the hot summer, Washington's forces were hurrying to their aid from the north and the French fleet had set sail for the Chesapeake.

Washington reached Chesapeake Bay early in September. There he was joined by the French under Rochambeau. The French fleet was also there, ready to carry the army into position around Yorktown. A total of 15,000 American and French troops laid siege to the British. Cornwallis made several attempts to break through, but he knew that he was beaten. On October 17, 1781, he surrendered his entire force.

3

Man of Peace

Benjamin Banneker looked to the future with great expectations. A new nation had been born in a spirit of liberty and justice. The war that won independence for America had brought about the personal liberty of about 100,000 slaves. Almost all the blacks who had served in the Army were given freedom for themselves and their families. Most of the slaves who had run away remained free, and thousands more were freed by owners who had caught the spirit of the Declaration of Independence.

That same spirit was reflected in many of the new state constitutions. Vermont abolished slavery outright; Pennsylvania's constitution called for gradual emancipation, extending the new freedom to those "who, though of a different color, are the work of the same Almighty hand." Within a few years Connecticut and Rhode Island adopted similar laws.

At the same time, however, proposals for gradual emancipation were rejected in every one of the Southern states. There the slaves were so numerous that to free them would change the whole economic and social system. Men were not ready for that change. Many slaveowners sincerely doubted the wisdom of emancipation. What would become of freed blacks? Must the owners give them land as well as liberty? How would they get along in a society convinced of white superiority? Southerners who were opposed to slavery decided not to wreck the system.

It was a different story in Massachusetts. The constitution of that state declared that "all men are born free and equal." Taking this to apply to himself, a twenty-eight-year-old slave named Quok Walker ran away and brought suit against his master. In a famous court decision the "born free" clause was applied, and slavery was finished in Massachusetts.

A similar court case ended slavery in New Hampshire for all those born after the decision was made. In New York a law was passed for gradual emancipation.

Like Quok Walker, Paul Cuffe of Boston appealed to the courts for his rights. A free son of an African slave, Cuffe was the builder and owner of several fine ships. Barely twenty-one years old, he owned and operated a shipping business and was subject to taxation in Massachusetts. "No taxation without representation" was the theme of the petition he placed before the Massachusetts court. Since he and other blacks were not allowed to vote, why should they pay taxes? The court ruled in Cuffe's favor and declared that all blacks subject to taxation should be allowed to vote.

Paul Cuffe became a Quaker and was deeply interested in the welfare of his black brothers. He was one of the first to favor their return to Africa and used his own ships to carry out this project. With his help, a small colony of ex-slaves set sail for the land of their forefathers.

Among whites as well as blacks, antislavery sentiments increased. Many abolition societies were organized, and men such as Benjamin Franklin, Benjamin Rush, Anthony Benezet, and Noah Webster did all they could to win others to their cause.

At Ellicott Mills, Benjamin Banneker was kept well informed of these activities. The general store had become the meeting place for the whole community. There all the best-informed local people gathered to discuss the news from various parts of the country. Banneker was always welcomed at these gatherings, and his clear and intelligent way of expressing his views won him great respect. Although he was already a man of fifty years, the greatest work of his life still lay ahead of him.

With his mother gone, Banneker now lived alone in his comfortable home. His two remaining sisters, Minta and Molly, lived nearby with their families and were able to help him with the domestic chores. Molly was married to Jim Morton, and their little son, Greenbury, loved to spend his afternoons with his Uncle Benjamin. There were frequent visits from neighboring friends, too, but long hours were spent in solitary study and thought.

By the terms of Joseph Ellicott's will, Banneker received many of his possessions. Among them were valuable instruments, books on astronomy, and a very fine telescope. These gifts opened up an entirely new world for the black man. His greatest interest in the years immediately following the war lay in the study of astronomy. He became so absorbed in his books that he had no interest in farming. Still, the land was his only source of income, and unless he farmed it he would have no money. He tried renting it out to tenant farmers, but this was not very successful. Finally he came to an agreement with George Ellicott. Banneker promised that upon his death his land would be willed to the Ellicotts. In exchange for the land, Ellicott agreed to pay Banneker a certain sum of money each year until his death. Banneker was to continue to live on the farm and use the land as he saw fit, but he would have enough money coming in so that he would not have to spend all his time farming.

Since both his sisters had enough land of their own, Banneker felt free to make this arrangement. However, he did hold back twenty-eight acres to be given to his favorite nephew, Greenbury Morton.

Now he had enough leisure to continue his studies. Astronomy was a very exacting science, and Banneker was no longer young, but he went about the work with such zeal and vigor of mind that he soon mastered it. His favorite method of studying was to lie flat on his back on the ground at night, looking at the heavens through his precious telescope.

His genius for mathematics was a great help to him. Among the books he was studying were Johann Mayer's *Tables*, James Ferguson's *Astronomy*, and Leadbetter's *Lunar Tables*. These authors were experts in the field, but Banneker found several mistakes in their calculations. He wrote a detailed letter to George Ellicott

showing what the errors were and telling how they
should be corrected. When this letter became public,
people were surprised to realize that a new astronomer
had appeared in western Maryland.

Compared to modern advances in astronomy, Banneker's work in this field seems rather small. But the
fund of human knowledge is built up bit by bit with
each man weighing, correcting, and adding to the work
of those who went before him. Each generation passes
on its work in order that the next generation may move
farther ahead. As a man of his times, Benjamin Banneker was a scientific genius.

The heavens fascinated him. He was impressed by
the immensity of the universe. "To us who dwell on its
surface, the earth is by far the largest orb," he wrote,
"but to a spectator placed on one of the other planets,
it is no larger than a spot. While beholding this vast
expanse I learn of my own littleness and of the littleness of all earthly things. What is the earth but a dim
speck hardly perceptible in the map of the universe?
What then is a kingdom or a country? When I take the
universe for my standard, how small are those wealthy
men who lord it over us! They shrink to pompous
nothings."

"What is a kingdom or a country?" What was the
new country of the United States in the year 1789 when
Banneker wrote those words?

The Articles of Confederation, which had bound the
various states together since the end of the war, had
not worked well at all. So in 1787 a convention was
called in Philadelphia to draw up a new constitution,
which eventually was ratified by all of the states.

The Constitutional Convention agreed that the new government "should rest on the dominion of property," but just exactly what was to be considered as property? Were slaves property or human beings?

The Southerners claimed that their slaves were property, to be bought and sold like animals or a piece of furniture. But such a view had its disadvantages. Representation in Congress was to be based on the population of each state. For this purpose, the Southerners wanted to count their thousands of slaves as human beings, thus gaining many more seats in the lower house.

In a shocking and absurd compromise, it was decided that each slave would be counted as three-fifths of a human being for representation purposes. Regarding his personal rights, he was considered as property!

Furthermore, under pressure from South Carolina and Georgia, the importation of slaves was allowed to continue for another twenty years.

Those whose lives were most affected, the 750,000 black Americans, had no voice at all in the decisions. Freeman and slave alike, they were forced to accept them.

George Washington became President of the United States of America, taking the oath of office in April, 1789. The next year Benjamin Franklin died.

Franklin's last public act was a memorial sent to Congress asking that liberty be restored "to those unhappy men, who alone, in this land of freedom, are degraded by perpetual bondage."

Statesman, scientist, and scholar, Benjamin Franklin had made many contributions to the life of Americans.

Not the least of these was *Poor Richard's Almanac*, which he published once a year, beginning in 1732. For many Americans, the almanacs were the only books they bought regularly and read carefully. With Franklin dead, *Poor Richard's Almanac* would be greatly missed.

Benjamin Banneker's friends urged him to write an almanac himself, saying that it would be an excellent way to use his knowledge of mathematics and astronomy. The idea interested Banneker, and he decided to try.

Almanacs were the scientific journals of that day. Farmers and seamen relied on them. By studying the sun and moon and all the laws of nature, scientists were able to forecast the weather a whole year in advance. They could tell the farmers what time the sun would rise and set on each day of the year and inform sailors and fishermen when the seas would be at low and high tide. This information was very important, because in those days there was no way of getting daily weather reports. Farmers planned their planting and harvesting by the almanac. Sailors used it in navigating. Travelers checked with it before going on a journey.

All this vital information had to be worked out scientifically on charts. It was exacting work, but Banneker was well suited to it. Benjamin Franklin's almanac had been full of wisdom, wit, and useful hints, as well as scientific information. Banneker's wide reading and remarkable memory made it possible for him to include many worthwhile comments and reflections in his own publication.

In 1791 the first almanac was ready. Its contents were

described on the first page: "the motions of the sun and moon, the true places and aspects of the planets, the rising and setting of the sun, the lunations, conjunctions, eclipses, judgments of the weather. Festivals and other remarkable days. Days for holding the Supreme Circuit Courts of the United States, as also the usual courts of Pennsylvania, Delaware, Maryland and Virginia; also several useful Tables and valuable recipes; various selections of the common-place Book of the Kentucky Philosopher, an American sage; with interesting and entertaining essays in prose and verse."

Banneker had predicted two solar eclipses for the year 1792. He also included the information that "needles were first made in London, by a Negro from Spain in the reign of Queen Mary."

The work drew the praise of James McHenry of Baltimore, who was to become a member of President John Adams' Cabinet. McHenry saw to it that the almanac was published. In a letter to the publisher, McHenry said he considered "this Negro as fresh proof that the powers of the mind are disconnected with the color of the skin" and that to imagine blacks were naturally inferior to whites was wrong. The publishers agreed. They published the almanac for its own merits, since it had been praised by several well-known astronomers, but in doing this they hoped that the work would help to combat the prejudice against the blacks.

This prejudice was very common in those days. Among the prominent men who held it was Thomas Jefferson, although he was a great champion of human rights for blacks as well as whites. Unlike Washington, who was content to express his hatred of slavery in words, Jefferson took direct action against the system on several occasions, proposing laws that would free the slaves. Yet abolition was only one of the many reforms with which he was concerned. Convinced that others had a right to their own opinion even when they disagreed with him, he sought to bring about social reform through legal means.

In 1791 Jefferson was Secretary of State for President Washington and had great influence in the country. Of all the statesmen of the day, he seemed to be the best equipped to take effective action in the fight against slavery. Benjamin Banneker decided to send him a copy of the new almanac. He hoped that it might correct his views on the mental capacities of his race. At the same time it would give Banneker a chance to voice his own horror at the way his fellow blacks were treated under slavery.

Banneker's famous letter to Thomas Jefferson was dated August 19, 1791. His tone was courteous and proper, but he spoke out clearly. He pointed out that all men have "one universal Father" and that though they may differ in society and religion, in situation or color, all are of the same family and stand in the same relation to Him. He told Jefferson that if he was sincere in his love of the rights of men he would do all he could to lift men up from the unjustifiable cruelty and barbarism of slavery.

"Sir," he wrote, "I freely and cheerfully acknowledge that I am of the African race, and in that color which is natural to them of the deepest dye. With profound gratitude to the Supreme Ruler I now confess to you that I am not under that state of inhuman captivity to which too many of my brethren are doomed. I have tasted the blessings of free and unequaled liberty."

Then he reminded Jefferson of how he himself had felt when he was under the tyranny of the British. "This, sir," he added, "was a time in which you clearly saw into the injustice of a state of slavery and knew the horrors of its condition; then it was that you set forth the true and valuable doctrine which is worthy to be recorded and remembered in all succeeding ages. 'We hold these truths to be self-evident, that all men are created equal, and that they are endowed by their Creator with certain unalienable rights, that among these are life, liberty and the pursuit of happiness.'"

He accused Jefferson of going against God's mercy and man's rights by "detaining by fraud and violence so numerous a part of my brethren under groaning captivity and cruel oppression," thus being guilty of the same criminal act which he detested in others.

He asked Jefferson to wean himself away from narrow prejudice and try to find some way to help the slaves gain their freedom.

With this letter, Banneker sent a handwritten copy of his almanac. Jefferson replied in a letter dated August 30, 1791. He wrote:

> Sir, I thank you sincerely for your letter and for the Almanac it contained. Nobody wishes more than I do to see such proofs as you exhibit that nature has given to our black brethren talents equal to those of the other colors of men, and that the appearance of a want of them is owing only to the degraded condition of their existence both in Africa and America. I can add with truth that no one wishes more ardently to see a good system com-

menced for raising the condition of their body and mind to what it ought to be as fast as the imbecility of their present existence and other circumstances which cannot be neglected will admit.

I have taken the liberty of sending your Almanac to Monsieur de Condorcet, Secretary of the Academy of Sciences at Paris and a member of the Philanthropic Society because I consider it a document to which your whole color had a right for their justification against doubts which have been entertained of them.

I am, with great esteem, sir, your most obedient servant,

Tho. Jefferson

Jefferson never said clearly what the "other circumstances" were which could not be neglected but which interfered with improving the condition of the slaves. However, history records that at the time of his death it was only by selling his slaves that the ex-President's debts could be paid.

True to his word, Thomas Jefferson sent Banneker's almanac on to Monsieur de Condorcet in Paris with a letter which said: "We now have in the United States a Negro . . . who is a very respectable mathematician. . . . He is a free Negro and is highly regarded in his community as a very worthy and respectable member of society. . . . I am sending this manuscript of his almanac to you."

Banneker's courage and loyalty to his race did not alter the cruel lot of the slaves, but his own merits were recognized by an ever-growing number at home and abroad. He received hundreds of letters of congratulations from scholarly men all over the world.

The year 1791 was most important in Banneker's life. Through his friend Major Andrew Ellicott he was appointed a member of the commission for laying out the new capital of the United States. Thomas Jefferson nominated him and the appointment came from George Washington, himself. Andrew Ellicott was also on the commission and the famous French engineer, Major Pierre Charles L'Enfant, was at its head.

President Washington suggested building an entirely new city in the district which lay along the Potomac River. This section was not far from his home of Mount Vernon, and he knew it well. It was mostly wooded land and included a village called George Town. In July, 1790, Congress made the territory on the Potomac federal property and the permanent seat of the government of the United States. Virginia and Maryland contributed land, and all was set for building to begin. The territory was called the District of Columbia and the city was to be named Washington, after the first President.

In March, 1791, Benjamin Banneker set out from Elk Ridge with Major Ellicott to undertake the planning of this new city. Their arrival in George Town was reported in the *Weekly Ledger* for March 12. It said that L'Enfant and Ellicott were accompanied by "Benjamin Banneker, an Ethiopian whose abilities as surveyor and astronomer already prove that Mr. Jefferson's concluding that that race of men were void of mental endowment was without foundation." Throughout the project, Banneker met with unfailing kindness and courtesy.

Major L'Enfant's idea was to place the capitol building on the highest hill in the district and lay out avenues around it like spokes from the hub of a wheel. The plan was similar to that of the beautiful city of Paris in his native France. But L'Enfant did not complete the work. After drawing up his plans he resigned from the commission. Ellicott took his place at the head and Banneker became his most prized assistant.

People who saw him at this time were impressed by his noble appearance: tall, benign, with thick white hair. His color was "not jet black, but decidedly Negro." He wore the broad-brimmed hat common among Quakers; though he never joined any church, he was much impressed by the Quaker religion and often went to the meetings of the Society of Friends in Elk Ridge.

Banneker was never a joiner. He had nothing to do with the Negro societies that were being formed in various cities, yet these societies were the first attempt of the black people to band together for the peaceful solution of the problems they faced.

The most famous society was one founded in Philadelphia by Richard Allen and Absalom Jones. In his youth, Allen had been a slave. Joining the Methodist Church, he became such a convincing preacher that he converted his own master and was permitted to buy his freedom in 1777. For several years, he preached to a mixed congregation of blacks and whites, but when the white people wanted to segregate the blacks in the balcony, he protested. He and his followers walked out of the church and founded their own. Allen became bishop of the African Methodist Episcopal Church.

Absalom Jones was an Angelican minister, but in spite of their religious differences, the two men worked together for the education and advancement of blacks. The society they founded was opposed to the plan that free blacks should leave the country and return to Africa. "We will never separate ourselves voluntarily from the slave population in this country," the members declared. The slaves were their brothers and they would rather suffer hardships with them than live free from prejudice in another land.

No doubt Banneker would have felt the same way. Yet if his own life during these years contained hardship and racial prejudice, no record of these has ever been found.

When his work in the District of Columbia was finished, he went back to his home near Ellicott Mills, returning to his study of astronomy and the writing of almanacs. Each year until 1802 he published a new almanac. His fame grew throughout the whole district, and many people came to visit him. Though he loved to be alone, he received them graciously. "His manners were those of a perfect gentleman," wrote one who visited him frequently, "kind, generous, dignified, and pleasing, abounding in information on all the various subjects and incidents of the day, and delighting in society at his own home."

Visitors were so impressed by his intellectual gifts that they seemed to give no thought to the question of his race. To them he was merely an honored citizen of great achievement who happened also to be black.

As he was now a renowned mathematician, he was constantly in correspondence with other mathematicians in the country, exchanging solutions to difficult problems.

But he had time for other studies besides mathematics. He had not forgotten his early days as a farmer, and since the farms around his home were sometimes plagued with locusts, he determined to study the problem. By proving that the locusts returned in cycles of seventeen years each, he was able to give advice on how to deal with the pests. He also wrote an interesting work on bees.

In the few hours that he allowed himself for recreation he usually turned to music. Sitting under the big chestnut tree on his hill, he would play simple tunes on his flute or violin.

The almanac was his way of attacking slavery. Through its pages Banneker was able to keep many readers informed of national and world opinion. The question of the slave trade came up in the English Parliament, and in fiery debates William Pitt and C. J. Fox spoke out for its abolition. "The greatest evil inflicted upon the human race," "the curse of mankind," "inhuman and unjust" were some of the terms they used to condemn this crime that "stained the honor of a country." All these speeches were faithfully recorded in Banneker's almanac to show white Americans what the "tyrant" England thought of the system they accepted.

England might abolish the slave trade, but in the United States the situation was becoming much worse. The invention of the cotton gin in 1793 made the slave system all the more necessary to the economic life of this country. The new machine could separate cotton fibers from the seeds quickly and easily. Unfortunately, however, it could not plant and pick the cotton itself.

For this backbreaking labor was required. Whose backs? Those of the black slaves.

In spite of state laws forbidding the importation of slaves, ships from New York and New England constantly brought black people from Africa and sold them in the Deep South. At first the laws were ignored; later many of them were repealed.

Slavery was not the only thing about American life that worried Benjamin Banneker in the year 1793. In Europe, England and France were again at war; and in the United States opinion was hotly divided on which nation this country should support. Thus the subject that concerned Banneker was peace. He came up with a unique plan for "promoting and preserving perpetual peace in our country" in the next edition of his almanac. The plan contained these seven ideas:

I   Let a Secretary of Peace be appointed who will be free from European prejudices upon the subject of government.

II   Let a power be given to this Secretary to establish and maintain free schools in every city, village and township in the United States and let him be responsible for all his schoolmasters.

III   Let every family be furnished at the public expense, by the Secretary, with a copy of the Bible.

IV   Let every home have a plaque reading: "The Son of Man came into the world not to destroy men's lives but to save them."

V   To inspire a veneration for human life and a horror for the shedding of human blood, let all those laws be repealed which authorize juries, judges, sheriffs, or hangmen to have the power to commit murder in cold blood in any case whatever.

VI   To subdue the passion for war, a familiarity with the instruments of death as well as all military shows should be avoided. Military dress and military titles should be laid aside.

VII   Let a large room be appointed for the business and records of the Secretary. Over the door should be painted the following letters of gold: "Peace on earth—good will to man. Ah! Why will men forget that they are brethren?"

Thomas Jefferson was President on the quiet afternoon in October, 1806, when Benjamin Banneker rested peacefully on the brow of his hill overlooking the Patapsco River valley. It was just before his seventy-fifth birthday. Almost a century had passed since the black prince Bannaky had looked out over the same lovely land.

Suddenly Banneker got up and started down the path. He had not gone far when he sank helplessly to the ground. By evening he was dead.

On the day of his death, his sisters Minta and Molly set about to carry out his wishes. All his notes, papers, books, and mathematical instruments were placed on the large table where he had worked for years. The table was put into a wagon, and Greenbury drove over to present the whole lot to George Ellicott. His letter to Thomas Jefferson together with the answer were there, too. This was done so quickly that the arrival of the things was the first sign Ellicott had that his good friend was dead.

By acting so promptly, Banneker's sisters saved all these valuable things for posterity, because two days afterward, during the funeral, Banneker's home caught fire and burned so rapidly that nothing could be saved.

The Federal Gazette and Baltimore Daily Advertiser carried the news: "On Sunday, the 25th instance, departed this life, near his residence in Baltimore County, Mr. Benjamin Banneker, a black man, immediately descended from an African father. He was well known in this neighborhood for his quiet and peaceful demeanor, and among scientific men as an astronomer and mathematician."

William Pitt placed his name in the records of the Parliament of England and the Marquis de Condorcet praised him before the Academy of Sciences in Paris.

Only in his own country did he go unhonored. Yet many years after his death—in 1863, when the country was torn by civil war—one writer had this to say of him:

Banneker died beloved and respected by all who knew him. Though no monument marks the spot where he was born, lived a true and high life, and was buried, history must record that the most original scientific intellect which the South has yet produced was that of the African, Benjamin Banneker.

Part II
Nat Turner and the Age of Violence

4
The Two Hundred Years' War

By the time Nat Turner was born, on October 2, 1800, a war between the black slaves and their owners had been going on for well over a century. In fact, the first recorded battle of the war took place in Turner's home state of Virginia in 1663. In a courageous bid for freedom, black slaves joined with white indentured servants to overthrow their masters, but the plot was betrayed by one of the white servants, and the rebels were put to death. Their bloody heads were displayed on the chimney tops of the town to warn any others who might be thinking of revolt.

With few differences, this story was to be repeated several hundred times in the next two hundred years. In some cases the black rebels were joined by white or Indian allies. In many cases there was a traitor who gave the plan away. Sometimes he was white, sometimes black. And almost always the slaveowners reacted by tightening their oppressive hold on their captive slaves.

Never was a war fought on such unequal terms. To begin with, the slaves were far outnumbered by the white people. In addition, the whites had all the wealth, the land, the weapons. The black slave had nothing but his own strength and his own desire for freedom.

Thousands of men, women, and children were held as prisoners of war, with no rights at all, forced to work all day so their white owners could live in luxury while they lived in misery. Under these conditions, many slaves lost heart, for constant cruelty can do terrible things to people. But others fought back, using whatever weapons they could find.

Wherever slavery existed revolts were plotted. In the South, where the slaves were numerous, their owners lived in constant fear of rebellion. If the system was to survive, the power of the master must be absolute; if the rebellious slaves were to be kept under control, an all-out policy of blood and iron must be adopted.

Behind the individual plantation owners stood local organizations of guards and patrols. And behind these stood the government militia. European visitors to the South were amazed by what they saw. Here was a military organization with more cruel power than any police state in Europe. "The fact is," one Englishman exclaimed, "they are all soldiers." Another visitor was shocked by the "military police constantly kept up." There can be little doubt that the South during slavery was in reality a military state.

Military control in the cities meant guards and police. In the country it meant constant patrols of armed men on horseback. It was the duty of these patrols to search "the hovels and hearts of the slaves for signs of rebellion," to catch and whip any blacks who were traveling without proper papers, to search out and disband any secret assemblies of slaves. Almost all adult white men were drafted for this patrol duty.

The full force of the law stood behind the organization. It was against the law for any slave to go off his own plantation without written permission. In the cities no slave was allowed on the streets after nine o'clock at night. There was a law against carrying weapons of any kind and one that forbade slaves to assemble without some white persons present. Laws prevented the slaves from buying, trading, or selling, from practicing medicine or testifying in court. Above all, it was against the law for any slave to lift his hand against a white man for any reason whatever. Often the penalty for this was death.

It was the duty of the guards and patrols to see that all these laws were kept and that no opportunity was given the slaves to unite.

The black men's strength lay in their unity. Knowing this, the slaveowners tried their best to keep their captives from communicating with one another. To weaken the solidarity of the slaves, those from the same African tribes were separated as far as possible. The field hands on the large plantations spoke so many different languages that uprisings and plots were difficult. Moreover, there was very little chance to unite with the slaves of neighboring plantations or to know what was going on in other camps of the slave army.

Above all, the slaves must not know what was going on. "I know it is the general opinion," wrote one white man, "that nothing ought to be published whereby the Negroes may be made acquainted with their own strength and the fear of danger the whites are in from them." Propaganda is an important part of any war, and the slaveowners used it to their own advantage.

They kept a careful censorship over news reports so that no one would know of all the plots and rebellions that took place among the slaves. They went out of their way to paint a picture of contented, well-treated blacks who would never dream of striking out against their dear masters.

True, there was a class of slave that fit this picture reasonably well. They were the house slaves, carefully picked to be the personal servants of the white family. Often these blacks would serve one member of the family for his or her entire life, and there can be no doubt that bonds of real affection grew between these slaves and their masters. Domestic servants were encouraged to hold themselves aloof from field workers. Living a life of comparative comfort and ease, these people felt closer to their white masters than to their black brothers. From this class came the spies and traitors who sold out their fellow slaves for the sake of a reward.

It was not in the white man's house but in the field hand's hut that the black rebels were born and raised. For every house servant, there were hundreds of these, toiling their lives away under the overseer's whip, looking for a chance to strike back.

Just as there were two types of slaves, there were two types of masters. Throughout the history of the slave South, there were always some slaveowners who worked for the reform of the system. These men treated their slaves with some degree of humanity and even affection. Often they allowed the blacks to buy their own freedom. But this group was only a small minority, caught in a web of fear, prejudice, and cruelty which held them helpless.

If the system was to be maintained, cruelty must be a part of it. Only through violence could the black man be forced to submit to his captors. Yet the picture that the slave South presented to the world was one of a peaceful life graciously lived, with carefree slaves sharing the comforts of plantation life, singing and laughing as they worked.

It was the white men who wrote the history of the South and they wrote it the way they pleased. But they did not have the last word. Scholars, both black and white, doing careful, difficult work and searching only for the truth, have uncovered another picture, very different from the one painted by the slaveowners. It is a picture of a brave people at war against their oppressors, determined to meet violence with violence.

Who were the unsung heroes in this undeclared war against slavery?

One of the first was a Maryland slave named Sam. Several times he tried to promote a rebellion among the slaves of his county, but in 1688 he was caught and convicted. He was severely beaten and forced to wear "a strong iron collar about his neck" with death as the penalty for removing it.

No names are given in the record of a small group of slaves on Long Island who rebelled early in 1708 and killed seven whites. Four slaves were executed, one woman burned to death.

The next year a large number of slaves organized for revolt in Virginia. The leaders were Tom Shaw,

Scipio, Salvadore, and Peter. Indians as well as black slaves were involved in the plot to escape by force from their masters and destroy anyone who opposed them. Scipio, Salvadore, and Tom Shaw were caught and punished, but Peter escaped. He was still free a year later when an award of ten pounds was offered for his capture alive and five pounds for his dead body.

A slave named Sebastian led a band of rebels in the spring of 1711. The people of South Carolina were "in great terror and fear" of these black men who were armed and kept "robbing and plundering houses and plantations." But finally Sebastian was tracked down and killed by a hunter, and nothing more was heard of his followers.

On the first day of 1712 a conspiracy was formed in New York City. The plotters bound themselves to secrecy by sucking the blood of each other's hands. A few months later about twenty-five or thirty of these slaves set fire to a building and, armed with clubs, knives, and a few guns, waited for the whites to approach. In the battle that followed, nine white men were killed and five or six others seriously wounded. Soldiers from a nearby fort hurried to the scene, and within twenty-four hours most of the rebels were captured. Some preferred death to capture and took their own lives. About seventy blacks were arrested. Twenty-one were put to death in the most cruel ways—some were burned, others hanged, one broken on the wheel, and one hung up alive in chains in the town.

Another serious plot was formed in South Carolina in 1720. The plan was to take the city of Charleston and destroy all the white people in the county. Once again, the plot was discovered and the rebels were taken prisoners and some burned, some hanged, some banished. Hardly a year passed without an explosion of this sort.

In 1722 Cooper Will and two slaves named Sam organized an uprising which covered two or three counties in Virginia. Although the rebels were crushed, by the very next year other Virginia slaves were again scheming to gain their freedom.

As the number of slaves increased, the number of plots and conspiracies also grew. Wherever black men were held in bondage throughout Colonial America, evidence of rebellion was uncovered. During the years between 1730 and 1741 the slave army attacked in South Carolina and Louisiana, Virginia and Maryland, New York, New Jersey, and Pennsylvania.

The greatest uprising of this period took place in Stono, South Carolina, about twenty miles from Charleston. There, on a Sunday evening, September 9, 1739, a small band of slaves attacked a warehouse. Killing two guards, they succeeded in capturing a store of small arms and ammunition.

Accounts differ concerning the leader of this band of rebels. Some say it was a slave named Jemmy; others claim that Cato organized the battle. Were there, perhaps, two leaders? No one will ever be sure.

Armed with the weapons from the warehouse and renewed with fresh courage, the rebels started down the road, headed for Florida and freedom. As they went, they set fire to several buildings so that "the country was full of flames." No white man they met escaped with his life except one, an innkeeper named Wallace.

He was spared because he was known to be "a good man and kind to his slaves."

Along the way the band was joined by other slaves until the little army had grown to seventy-five or eighty. Someone hoisted a flag, two drums beat out a marching rhythm, and the slaves pushed on, shouting "liberty, liberty" as they went.

By chance, the lieutenant-governor of the province happened to be riding near the line of march. As soon as he saw what was going on, he spread the alarm.

The white army swung into action. Guards were posted at all the ferries and roads; the militia was called up and sent out in pursuit. Meanwhile the blacks pushed on, but after marching and fighting for ten or twelve hours, they stopped to rest about ten miles south of Stono. There they were overtaken and attacked by the militia.

In the pitched battle that followed the slaves fought bravely but were defeated. The militia killed fourteen of them on the spot. Twenty more were killed in battle within the next few days, and forty prisoners were taken. Of the prisoners, some were immediately shot and others hanged.

Pursuit of the remaining rebels continued for several months, and before the uprising had been completely stamped out, twenty-five whites and at least twice as many slaves had been killed.

Far from frightening the other slaves, the rebellion at Stono spurred them on. A few months later a plot was uncovered in Charleston involving about two hundred slaves. A traitor had given the slaveowners advance warning of the plan, so that an armed force was ready when the trouble started. On the day of the outbreak, fifty blacks were caught. These were hanged in batches of ten a day in an effort to frighten other slaves. But the slaves were not to be stopped. Later that same year terrible fires broke out in Charleston, the work of defiant blacks bent on destroying the entire town.

After 1741 there was an uneasy truce which lasted for the next fifty years. The number of organized rebellions was much fewer, but just why this was true no one knows. Perhaps in these years of prosperity the lot of the slave was not quite so hard to endure. Perhaps the furious activity of the preceding years and the brutality with which the rebellions had been put down made the next generation of slaves more cautious. In any case, complete quiet did not prevail. There continued to be minor uprisings in Maryland, Virginia, and South Carolina during these years.

At the same time, other forms of resistance and rebellion continued. Plotting revolt was by no means the only way of fighting in the war against slavery. Poisoning was quite common. In two places slaves managed to poison the water supply. Setting fire to plantation houses and outbuildings was another method, used so often that it was almost impossible for Southern planters to take out fire insurance. Refusing to work, pretending to be sick, and sabotage were all ways used by the black man to show he would not submit to the white man's tyranny.

Still, for the freedom-loving slave the most direct method of escaping slavery was to run away. During the Two Hundred Years' War, countless black men made a break for it. They ran to any place where freedom was possible. They went to the Spaniards, the Mexicans, the Canadians, the Indians. They went to mountains, forests, and swamps.

Those fugitives who took refuge in the forests and swamps of Colonial America banded together in small groups and were known as the Maroons. From their hiding places they made guerrillalike attacks on plantations in the surrounding area, causing considerable damage to the owners and stealing those supplies necessary to maintain their fugitive camps. These camps became places of refuge for other fleeing slaves.

One of the early Maroon leaders was a slave named Mingoe. He and his band ravaged a number of Virginia plantations in 1691 and succeeded in capturing guns as well as livestock. Some years later, in 1729, a large number of slaves ran off to the Blue Ridge Mountains of Virginia, taking with them guns, ammunition, and farming tools. A small community was set up, and for a while it looked as though it might prosper. However the whites were quick to see what a great threat such a community would be to slavery as a whole. A strong body of armed men was sent out to attack the settlement, and after a pitched battle the few remaining blacks were led back to bondage.

Since Florida was under Spanish rule, it was a haven for runaway slaves all during the eighteenth century. This was especially true after the year 1733, when a decree was issued that all fugitives reaching there would be allowed to live as free people. Great numbers, particularly from South Carolina, succeeded in crossing the border to liberty, and a colony of freedmen grew up near St. Augustine. The fort built by these blacks served as a beacon pointing the way for other fugitives.

In spite of all efforts to wipe out Maroon camps, new groups kept springing up all over America.

In the fight against slavery, the system was the enemy and freedom was the prize to be won. If the white man sided with the system against the slave, he became the enemy; if he was willing to join forces against oppression, he became an ally.

Such phrases as "Give me liberty or give me death," spoken by white men, fanned the flames of rebellion in the hearts of American slaves.

A few miles off the coast of Florida, on the island of Santo Domingo, similar words were being spoken. The French Revolution raised the battle cry "Liberty, Fraternity, Equality." Santo Domingo, a French island possession in the Caribbean, had a huge slave population, and these words spread through the country like wildfire.

No mounted patrols stopped the island slaves as they followed the beat of the drums deep into the woods to speak of freedom. Under cover of night, they came from all the plantations for miles around to lay their plans and set the date when liberty would become a reality.

That day came on August 22, 1791. In an instant, more than 100,000 slaves rose up in revolt, burning, murdering, and plundering. Within a few weeks, 1,200 plantations went up in flames, and clouds of smoke hung over the whole northern part of the island.

The French government called out the militia, and in the fierce fighting that followed 2,000 whites and almost 10,000 blacks were killed. The rebels took refuge in the hills while the militia patrolled the plains, killing all the blacks they could find. Thousands who had not intended to join the revolt were forced to flee from the militia to the rebel camp.

There in the wooded hills the blacks were joined by the man who was to become their leader and the father of the Haitian Republic. His name was Toussaint L'Ouverture.

Nothing in his appearance marked him as a leader. Only five feet two inches tall, very black, with large eyes, thick lips, and a long, pointed chin, he was not handsome by any standard. His kinky hair was graying, for he was already fifty years old. Yet the man was a military genius. Holding a musket high in his hand, he shouted to the rebel blacks, "Here, here is your liberty!"

Toussaint's first task was to form a disciplined army out of the bands of rebels. He seemed to work miracles. Those who saw him in action said he had the fierce energy of a tiger. The whole camp loved him and would obey his least command. Soon he had organized a corps of expert and well-disciplined fighting men that amazed the white foe.

Determined that the slaves should remain free at any cost, Toussaint became the ally of the Spanish against the French. Then, as the fortunes of war changed, he sided with the French against England and Spain. Playing the Spanish against the French and the French against the English, he managed to gain control of the entire island.

American slaveowners trembled for their own safety as they followed the revolutionary activities of Toussaint. Fearful that the revolt would spread to the United

States, many slept with guns at their sides and carried their weapons everywhere.

As news of one victory after another reached their ears, the Americans were forced to take notice of the ex-slave who had defied the great powers of Europe. Though the French still claimed possession of Santo Domingo, Toussaint was actually the military and political ruler of the whole island, which he called Haiti, restoring the original Indian name. In 1799 the United States government decided to come to terms with him and recognized him as the head of the government. Toussaint was offered economic support if he would guarantee that no persons dangerous to the slave regions of the United States would be allowed to leave his island. Toussaint kept his part of the bargain.

By 1801 Toussaint was ready to try his strength against the most powerful ruler of the day. Napoleon Bonaparte, before whom all Europe had bowed, was now Emperor of France. Napoleon was determined to crush the "insolent old Negro" and restore slavery to Santo Domingo. He marshaled a huge military force and sent it to invade the island of Haiti in the name of France. In the bloody war that followed, Toussaint was captured and sent to die in a French prison, but his followers fought on until the mighty army of Napoleon was driven from the island. On January 1, 1804, the Republic of Haiti was officially proclaimed.

If Toussaint struck terror in the hearts of white Americans, he sparked courage in the souls of their slaves. Stories of his colorful life were told in slave quarters throughout the South, and the blacks renewed their efforts to break the chains that bound them to their white masters. But the Haitian blacks had advantages that those in the United States did not have. In Haiti there were more blacks than whites. In America it was the other way around. And the blacks in this country were spread out over thousands of miles with very little means of communication. The many uprisings remained small and local in character.

The most important rebellion of this period took place in Virginia under the leadership of Gabriel Prosser, a slave on a plantation near Richmond. He was twenty-four years old in the spring of 1800 when he started planning his fight for freedom. Described as "a fellow of courage and intellect above his rank in life," Prosser was six feet two inches tall and wore his black hair long in the style of the Old Testament prophets. These same prophets were his heroes and the source of his inspiration.

He laid his plans carefully. Each Sunday he went into Richmond to talk to the black people and make recruits. He scouted around until he had located all arms and ammunition stored in the city and knew the lay of the land by heart. During the week he quietly enlisted men from the nearby plantations.

At a secret meeting George Smith and Jack Bowler were chosen as second in command. "We have as much right to fight for our liberty as any men," Bowler told the others. Prosser's wife, Nanny, was also active in the plot, together with his brothers, Solomon and Martin. Solomon was in charge of making swords and bayonets to arm the men. Five hundred bullets were also made by the slaves, who donated what little money they had to buy gunpowder. Ben Woolfolk, another of the band, went into North Carolina to recruit more slaves from there.

"Death or Liberty" was the motto of these courageous black men. They planned to inscribe the words on a silk flag and carry it into battle. They knew the odds were against them, but they were desperate men willing to die for their cause.

As the day set for the attack drew near, the number of slaves enlisted in the plot reached several thousands. Nearly all the blacks in Richmond had joined, free men and slaves alike. The leaders planned to begin at the Prosser plantation, killing the white men with swords and scythe blades. At a nearby tavern, they hoped to capture some guns and ammunition, and thus armed they would march on to Richmond.

In the city, Bob Cooley and Tim Tinsley had agreed to let them into the capitol building, where a large supply of arms was stored. The forces were divided into three columns. One section would seize the guns, another the powder house. The third group was assigned to set fire to the lower part of the city to draw all the white people to that section while the blacks seized the arms and ammunition. Then the entire city would be attacked.

All white men were to be killed except Quakers, Methodists, and Frenchmen. Once Richmond had been taken, the black army would secure itself against attack from without and would do battle against other Virginia towns. If the plan succeeded, Gabriel Prosser would be named King of Virginia. If it failed, the band would take to the woods, where it could keep up guerrilla warfare.

For months these plans had been carefully guarded, but on August 30, the very day set for the revolt, two slaves, Tom and Pharoah, betrayed the plot to their master. He quickly informed the governor of Virginia, James Monroe, later to be President of the United States.

Governor Monroe lost no time in taking action. He called into service more than 650 men, posted cannon in Richmond, and gave notice of the plot to every militia commander in the state.

Besides Tom and Pharoah there was another traitor— the weather. Just at sunset on the fateful Saturday a terrible thunderstorm broke over the countryside. Rain came down in the worst storm anyone in the neighborhood had ever seen. Gabriel met with his men and decided that the attack would have to be postponed until the next day. They did not know that they had been betrayed and that the delay would give the state troops valuable time to prepare for action.

The next day, Sunday, 1,000 slaves gathered for the attack. Some were mounted on horses. A few had guns. Others carried clubs, scythes, or homemade swords and bayonets. But as they advanced on Richmond they found that the only bridge that they could take to the city was completely washed out by the storm. At this point the band was attacked by the white militia, and although they tried to defend themselves, they were forced to disband and run.

The white army of the slave state had gone into action, and in the next few days dozens of blacks were arrested. Gabriel Prosser fled to Norfolk and tried to get away by sea, but on September 23 he was caught and brought back to Richmond in chains. James Monroe questioned him in person. A former rebel himself, the governor was deeply impressed by the character and ideals of the black man. "From what he said to me," the future President reported, "he seemed to have made up his mind to die, and to have resolved to say but little on the subject of the conspiracy."

Monroe wrote to Thomas Jefferson asking his advice concerning the fate of the rebels. Jefferson warned him against seeking revenge, saying that he must "not lose sight of the rights of the two parties and the object of the unsuccessful one." As a result, ten of the condemned slaves were given a reprieve and banished. Nevertheless, Gabriel Prosser was sentenced to hang along with at least thirty-five others.

The bravery of the condemned men won praise from their white captors. One wrote, "Of those who have been executed, no one has betrayed his cause. They have uniformly met death with fortitude." Another said, "The accused have exhibited a spirit which, if it becomes general, must deluge the Southern country with blood. They show a sense of their rights and a contempt for danger and a thirst for revenge."

To Gabriel Prosser tradition has assigned the words that sum up the spirit of this band of revolutionaries. When asked if he had anything to say in his defense, he said, "I have nothing more to offer than what George Washington would have had to offer had he been taken by the British and put to trial by them. I have adventured my life in endeavoring to obtain the liberty of my countrymen and am a willing sacrifice to their cause; and I beg, as a favor, that I may immediately be led to execution. I know that you have predetermined to shed my blood. Why then all this mockery of a trial?"

Gabriel Prosser was hanged October 7, 1800. On October 2, while he was awaiting death, a child was born only a few miles away in Southampton County, Virginia. This child was the true heir of Gabriel's great spirit. His name was Nat Turner.

5

The Growing Years

A story was told about the birth of Nat Turner: His mother had been born in Africa and brought to America on a slave ship. With the memory of her lost freedom still in her mind and heart, she could not bear the thought that her son should live the life of a slave. The very idea of it filled her with such rage that she had to be tied down to prevent her from murdering her infant son.

Nat took his last name from his master, Benjamin Turner, who owned a large plantation in Southampton County, Virginia, where he and his parents were slaves. But it was from his own father and mother that he inherited his passion for freedom. Another story told about him was that his parents soon became convinced their baby boy was intended for some great purpose.

Still another story told about Nat was that he became convinced of his own great destiny at a very early age. When he was three or four years old and talking with some other children, his mother happened to overhear what he was saying and was amazed. Nat was describ-

ing things that had happened before he was born,
things he could not possibly know in a natural way!
She questioned the child, but he stuck to his story and
even added more details. When she called her friends
and relatives to listen to this amazing tale, all agreed
that Nat was telling these things just as they had happened. They all said he would surely be a prophet.

As he grew older, his parents saw that he was very
intelligent and wanted to give him the best education
possible. Although there were no schools, the slave
society could teach him many valuable things that he
could never learn from books. But his parents wanted
him to learn to read and write too. They taught him
themselves, and the little boy proved such a bright pupil
that once more they were amazed. He found learning
so easy that in later life he could not recall learning the
alphabet. He only remembered the day when his family
gave him a book to keep him from crying and he began
spelling the names of different objects. This was another
source of wonder to the black community. They claimed
he had too much sense to be raised as a slave.

Nat's grandmother also played an important part in
his education. She was a very religious woman, and
Nat was especially fond of her. She owned only one
book, the Bible, which she knew practically by heart.
She and Nat spent many hours pondering over the
sacred texts. Together these two, the old woman and
the young boy, read the book over and over again.

His parents' passionate love of freedom and his grandmother's deep love of the Christian religion met and
became one in this remarkable child.

The black Christianity that Nat Turner learned from

his grandmother and others of the slave community was unique. Although the slaves had been introduced to the teaching of Christ by their white slavemasters, these teachings had a special meaning for them. They saw the basic contradiction between what the whites taught and the way they lived. Though they were uneducated, they went straight to the heart of the matter, to the real meaning and substance of Christianity.

Christ, they believed, was a true revolutionary who spoke out against the system and condemned the religious leaders who taught one thing and did the opposite. True, those same leaders put Him to death on the cross, but it was He who triumphed. Out of suffering came new life in the glorious resurrection. The slaves knew by their own experience just what the Cross of Christ meant. They knew that slavery was completely opposed to everything for which Christ stood. Their God had cursed man-stealers, had led the slaves out of bondage. He had promised that the first would be last and the last first. He had promised that the humble would inherit the earth. The Christian message proclaimed the fatherhood of God and the brotherhood of men—all men, regardless of race or social position. Nat Turner grew up in a community of religious rebels.

Religion was by no means the only thing that interested young Nat. He was a keen observer of everything that went on around him and made the best use of each opportunity to increase his knowledge and satisfy his lively curiosity. Since he was a slave, there were not many books available to him, but he said later, "Whenever an opportunity occurred of looking at a book, when the white school children were getting their lessons,

I would find many things that the fertility of my own imagination had depicted to me before."

Thomas Jefferson, author of the Declaration of Independence and champion of human rights, was still President in 1807 when Congress finally passed a law prohibiting the slave trade. The inhuman system that had brought one million Africans to American shores was brought to an end. Zeal for human rights had little to do with the decision. White men were afraid to have the black population increased. They lived in fear of black insurrections.

Attempts to keep the black people uninformed were not very successful. One Southerner reported, "The Negroes have a wonderful art of communicating intelligence among themselves; it will run several hundreds of miles in a week or a fortnight." Efforts to prevent secret meetings met with the same fate. Under cover of night, the slaves crept off to "hush harbors," where they sang hymns and plotted rebellion. Such meetings were an important part of Nat Turner's upbringing.

There he learned of a growing community of Maroons in nearby North Carolina. These runaway slaves banded together into an outlaw guerrilla army had "defied any force whatever, and were resolved to stand their ground." In March, 1811, armed white men set upon the community, determined to wipe it out. In the battle, two blacks were killed, more wounded and some captured.

The story was told of a slave named Tom who had killed his master and fled. He was caught and forced to confess. Tom said that he knew of about forty slaves who were making plans for a rebellion under a leader named Goomer of Rockingham County, North Carolina.

These slaves said "they were not created to work for white men, but the white people were meant to work for themselves and that they [the blacks] would have it so." When Tom told a slave woman of these plans, she said "they could not rise too soon for her, as she would rather be in hell than where she was." What finally became of Goomer and his fellow rebels is not known.

While the Southern states struggled to keep their slaves under control, the nation moved closer to a second war with Great Britain. The British, already at war with Napoleon, were using their large navy to prevent the United States from trading with Europe and the West Indies, even though this country had declared its neutrality. British cruisers patrolled the coastline, while British sailors boarded and searched American vessels, forcing American seamen into service under the British flag. At the same time the British stirred up the Indians against the American frontier.

Defeated on land and blockaded by sea, the Americans were close to disaster by 1813 when they set to work building a fleet of ships to fight in the Great Lakes. Using black and white workmen, the ships were completed in record time, but no sailors were available to man them. Captain Oliver H. Perry, who was in command, complained to the Navy Department that he had no one except "blacks, soldiers and boys." In answer, Commodore Isaac Chauncey claimed that Perry should be glad to have the blacks, saying, "They are not surpassed by any seamen we have in the fleet. . . . I have nearly fifty blacks on board this ship, and many of them are among my best men."

Chauncey proved to be right. With a crew that was

one-fourth black, Perry attacked the British fleet in Lake Erie. The fierce fighting that followed ended in the only surrender of a complete British squadron in the naval history of that country.

Perry reported the victory in the famous words, "We have met the enemy and they are ours." He also had a special word of praise for his black seamen. "They seemed absolutely insensible to danger," he marveled.

Black men were also fighting on land and on ships in the Atlantic. Although slaves were definitely excluded from service, many free blacks fought bravely.

Slaveowners in Georgia were worried about events in East Florida, where fugitive slaves joined with the Indians in carrying on guerrilla warfare against them. In the far-off Mississippi Territory the dread of slave rebellion was very great. The governor sent a plea for additional arms, saying, "Scarcely a day passes without my receiving some information relative to designs of these people to insurrect."

All during the War of 1812 the war against slavery continued. Hundreds of blacks escaped to the wilderness. Revolts and rumors of revolt filled the South.

Near the end of the war the British launched an attack against New Orleans with a large force. General Andrew Jackson, who would later become President, accepted slavery as an "institution" in his state of Tennessee. But when it came to the defense of New Orleans he said he did not care whether his troops were black, white, or "tea-colored."

He issued a proclamation to all free blacks: "As sons of freedom, you are now called upon to defend our most inestimable blessing." He directed that blacks were to receive the same pay as white soldiers and noncommissioned officers were to be chosen by them. Hundreds of blacks enlisted in response to his call.

Black fought black in the Battle of New Orleans. The British forces included hundreds of soldiers from Haiti, as well as many slaves who had fled to the British lines in search of freedom.

In the final British attack on the city more than 2,000 British soldiers were killed, including their commander, General Edward Pakenham. Commenting on the general's death, Jackson wrote, "I have always believed he fell from a bullet of a free man of color, who was a famous rifle shot and came from the Attakaps region of Louisiana."

With their general dead, the remaining British troops withdrew, only to learn that the costly battle need never have been fought. Although neither side had received the news, the War of 1812 had already been over for two weeks. A treaty had been signed between the British and the Americans at Ghent, Belgium, December 14, 1814.

In the slave South the struggle for freedom went on. Late in 1815 George Boxley, a white man, organized the slaves in Virginia to revolt. The rebels were to meet at Boxley's house with whatever horses and weapons they could find. The plan was to attack Fredericksburg first and then move on to Richmond, but a black woman betrayed the plot and military forces crushed the rebels. Thirty slaves were arrested, six hanged. Boxley himself escaped and went into hiding.

This was the background of the times in which Nat Turner grew up. Once he became old enough to work, he had to spend long hours in his master's service, but he found time to pray and read. His sense of mission grew steadily, and he became a leader among his black brothers. Even at an early age he was plotting and organizing his fellow slaves in resistance against slavery, according to later testimony.

One form of resistance was stealing. Since a slave worked all day, year after year, for no pay at all, many a one felt he had a right to share in the wealth his labor produced; he felt the only share he would ever have would be what he was able to take by stealth. To a man who had been robbed of his freedom, it was foolish to claim he should not steal from the robbers who had enslaved him. In the mind of a slave, a slaveowner was the worst kind of thief—a man-stealer.

So Nat went along with his gang, planning their raids on the enemy's gardens and storehouses and giving the others confidence because of his courage and good judgment. At the same time, oddly, he had a reputation for honesty. One later report stated, "From childhood Nat was very religious, truthful and honest, never owning a dollar, never uttering an oath, never drinking intoxicating liquors, and never committing a theft."

It was about this time that Nat's father ran away to the North. The exact circumstances surrounding his escape are not known and he never was heard from again. Nat left the Turner plantation and became the slave of Putnam Moore.

Who can say what Nat Turner might have become if he had lived in a different age and received a formal education? His thirst for knowledge was never satisfied. Although he never had the proper equipment to carry

out his experiments, he managed to become well informed on how to make paper and gunpowder.

As he grew older Nat became increasingly certain
that God had chosen him for a special mission. He
spent more time in fasting and prayer and did not take
much part in the social life of his fellow blacks.

One day he was praying as he worked at his plow
when the spirit spoke to him, saying, "Seek ye first the
kingdom of Heaven and all things will be added unto
you."

He was astonished. He felt that this was the same
spirit that had spoken to the prophets of old. But what
was the meaning of the message? For two years he
continued to pray, asking God for guidance. Again he
heard the same message.

Nat Turner was sixteen years old when the American
Colonization Society was organized to ship free blacks
to Africa. Back-to-Africa schemes had been proposed
before by both black and white men, and a few blacks
had even made the trip. Many antislavery people supported it, thinking it was an answer to the problem of
slavery. Others saw it as a way to rid the country of
free blacks who were considered to be dangerous.

Most black people opposed the plan. "This is our
home," they felt in effect, "and this is our country. Be-
neath its soil lie the bones of our fathers; for it some
of them fought, bled, and died. Here we were born
and here we will die." Others welcomed the return to
the land of their ancestors. One of these wrote, "We
love this country and its liberties; but our freedom is
partial, and we have no hope that it ever will be other-

wise here; therefore we had rather be gone, though we suffer hunger and nakedness for years."

Black people spoke eloquently, but white people made the decisions. Madison's successor, President James Monroe, also supported the back-to-Africa plan. In 1817 the United States signed a treaty with the native tribes of West Africa and was granted a tract of land at the mouth of St. Paul River. A small community of blacks set sail, land was cleared, and a settlement was established. The new republic was named Liberia, and its capital city was called Monrovia, after President Monroe.

Throughout these years activities in the Florida border were keeping the slave population in a restless and rebellious state. The Spanish in Florida continued to help fugitive blacks in any way they could and often enlisted them as soldiers. Runaway slaves found a haven in the swamplands, and banding together with the Seminole Indians, they made lightninglike attacks on the plantations across the border.

By 1818 the Southern slaveowners had had enough. General Andrew Jackson was sent into the territory with a military force, and the next year Spain ceded Florida to the United States in exchange for five million dollars.

However, the hostile blacks and Indians were not to be stopped. For the next twenty years their activities kept the territory in a state of turmoil.

Now the slavery issue loomed large in national politics. Ever since the Constitution had been adopted there had been a balance of power between the slaveholding states of the South and the Northern states where slavery was forbidden. In the Westward rush which fol-

lowed the War of 1812, thousands of slaveowners mi-
grated to the territory of Missouri, where wheat and cotton plantations sprang up. When these people demanded admission to the Union as a state, slavery was
permitted by their proposed constitution.

The question of slavery in Missouri was discussed
throughout the country. The debate, which was long
and bitter, centered around sectional power. Finally a
compromise was reached. Missouri was admitted as a
slaveholding state, but slavery was prohibited in the territory farther north. At the same time, Maine was given
statehood, thus giving each section twelve states. That
was in 1820.

The following year Nat Turner reached his twenty-
first birthday. Most of his life had been spent in preparing himself for what he felt was a great mission. Now
the time had come to prepare his people. He had already become a man of importance in the county, and
his fellow slaves looked to him for advice and direction.
Black and white alike recognized his exceptional abilities.

He was not tall, but he had broad, powerful shoulders. His African features and large dark eyes gave him
a bold and commanding look. He was virile, keen, and
courageous. Although he had never received a formal
education, he was highly intelligent, well-informed, and
mechanically gifted. His companions viewed him with
awe. His manner of life impressed them and they believed that his wisdom came from God. Many blacks
called him the Prophet.

He would often talk to them of the things which the
spirit had made known to him. Later he said, "I now

began to prepare them for my purpose by telling them something was about to happen that would fulfill the great promise that had been made to me."

As Turner took his place of leadership in the community in Southampton County, another black revolutionary was planning one of the most serious and widespread of all the plots against slavery. This man was Denmark Vesey. Vesey had been born in Africa but was sold into slavery when he was just a young man. His master was a slave trader, and Vesey spent twenty years aboard a slave ship. He had traveled widely and learned several languages. But the things he saw aboard that ship convinced him that slavery was one of the greatest of all evils. He had such contempt for white slaveowners that he could not even stand to have a white person in his presence.

Eighteen hundred, the year Gabriel Prosser was hanged and Nat Turner was born, was also an important time in the life of Denmark Vesey. By a lucky chance he won a lottery and with it enough to buy his freedom. As a freeman, he moved to Charleston, South Carolina, where he became a carpenter. He made money, purchased some good property, and was respected by white and black alike. He had to admit that he was satisfied with his own conditions, yet he could not live content as long as his black brothers were enslaved.

This brilliant, freedom-loving man was willing to risk everything he had to gain the freedom of other men. When he was offered a chance to move to Africa he refused to go. He said that he wanted to stay and see what he could do to help the slaves.

Slowly and carefully he started making his plans. For four or five years he went around agitating among the slaves. When he saw slaves bowing to a white man he would scold them. When they replied, "But we are slaves," he would answer with scorn, "You deserve to be slaves."

At this point the usual response of the slave was, "But what can we do?" Vesey had the opening he wanted, and before long he had made a recruit.

He seemed never to rest. Always, everywhere, he was teaching and agitating. His method was direct. He met one of his prospective recruits with the question, "What's new?"

The slave answered, "Nothing."

Vesey replied, "We are free, but the people here won't let us be so, and the only way is to rise up and fight the whites."

He carried with him antislavery articles and newspaper reports about the Haitian Revolution. Whenever he got a chance he would read these to any slave who seemed interested. The number of his followers increased by leaps and bounds.

In 1821 he chose his chief aides and set up his organization. Vesey was the only freeman in the plot. Though they were slaves, the other leaders were tradesmen from the city—carpenters, harnessmakers, mechanics and blacksmiths. Vesey, in his middle fifties, was himself the oldest of the group. Little is known of his personal appearance except that he wore a beard.

He chose his aides well. Chief among them was Peter Poyas, a first-rate ship's carpenter with a genius for organization. He was cool-headed and fearless, but he was also cautious. He warned against recruiting house servants, saying, "Take care and don't mention this to those waiting men who receive presents of old coats and the like from their masters, or they'll betray us."

Mingo Harth was another trusted leader. Rollo and Ned Bennett were described as men of "firm nerves and desperate courage" and not to be stopped by any fear of danger. Gullah Jack, an African-born sorcerer, had a great influence on the slaves who still believed in witchcraft. He was thought to have supernatural powers.

Vesey, too, was a religious man. At the secret meetings of the plotters he read from the Bible, especially the part where the children of Israel were delivered from bondage out of Egypt. The plans were discussed.

Every store that contained arms was marked. All slaves who could get horses were told where to bring the animals and when. A barber was assigned to make wigs and whiskers to disguise the rebels. Two hundred and fifty bayonets and over three hundred daggers were made.

The slave army was to strike at five points at once, with a sixth division on horseback patrolling the streets. The fearless Peter Poyas volunteered for the most dangerous task. He was to advance alone into the main guardhouse, surprise the guard, and slit his throat. Then he would open the gates for the rest of his unit to enter. All whites were to be killed, for the motto of the blacks was "He that is not with me is against me."

Recruits had been made throughout Charleston and the surrounding country. Sometimes whole plantations were signed up. It has been said that 9,000 slaves were involved in the plot. July 16, 1822, was the date set for the revolt.

But Peter Poyas' warning against house slaves was not heeded by one of the plotters. On May 25, he tried to recruit a favorite slave of Colonel Prioleau, and this slave immediately betrayed the plot to his master. As a result, Peter Poyas and Mingo Harth were arrested, but these brave men "behaved with such composure and coolness that the wardens were completely deceived." Both were set free, but spies were set to follow them.

A few days later another traitor went over to the enemy. This one, a black named William, was able to give details of the plan. The whole city was alerted and the authorities quickly acted to arrest the rebels. One hundred and thirty-one blacks were taken prisoner and forty-nine were condemned to death.

Denmark Vesey and most of the leaders were among those sentenced to die. Only one man among them confessed. The rest refused to talk. Peter Poyas set the example. "Do not open your lips," he said. "Die silent as you shall see me do."

Those rebels who were not captured tried desperately but unsuccessfully to rescue the prisoners. Even on the day of Vesey's execution, the slaves rose up, "so determined to strike a blow for liberty that it was found necessary for the federal government to send soldiers to maintain order."

Like Gabriel Prosser before him, Vesey was betrayed by one of his own men. He died a martyr for the cause of freedom for his black brothers.

6

"Nat's Fray"

News of Denmark Vesey's plot spread quickly by the slaves' secret communication system. Slaves in all parts of the South were spurred on by the hope that next time the strike for freedom would succeed. The period that followed was one of great activity in the slave army that was to grow to a climax in Nat Turner's revolt of 1831.

Fear was growing, too, among the slaveowners of the South. New laws were added to the long list of oppressive measures that bound the black man under the yoke of bondage. Many of these were directed against free blacks and city slaves, since it was from among these groups that the leaders of the Vesey revolt had come. Laws were passed prohibiting the hiring-out of slaves, and it became a crime to teach any black man to read or write. Every free black over fifteen years old was required to have a "guardian" who would "control his behavior." More laws kept blacks from gathering together, and patrol regulations became more severe.

Freedom-loving people throughout the world were

97

shocked, and opposition to the institution of slavery grew. As people from Europe and the Northern states began to agitate against this evil system, the Southern slaveowners sought to justify their position. Every possible field of human knowledge—religion, science, history—was twisted and used in support of their view that, far from being an evil, slavery was a "positive good." Books and articles were written claiming that the black race was better off in bondage and needed a master to support and control it. Ministers, teachers, and politicians who disagreed with this view were eliminated from power.

In the White House James Monroe continued his efforts to colonize the blacks in far-off Africa. Was he ever haunted by the thought of the tall, fiery revolutionary, Gabriel Prosser, whom he had interviewed in 1800? Was he troubled by the frequent news of plots and revolts in his home state of Virginia? Did he know that each one proclaimed once more the "self-evident" truths of his country's Declaration of Independence?

As a youth Monroe himself had been a revolutionary and a "radical," but age had made him more conservative. He was more concerned with America's relations with other countries than with race relations inside its borders. In 1823, with the help of his Secretary of State, John Quincy Adams, he published his Monroe Doctrine, which was to be the official policy of the United States for many years to come.

Taking the same stand as Washington and Jefferson, Monroe stated that the United States would not become involved in any European war; neither would she interfere with any existing European colony in the Western

Hemisphere. However, she would not permit further colonization by any power or allow the politics of Europe to be extended to this hemisphere.

In the "Era of Good Feeling" that marked Monroe's eight years as President, the political and social life of America was outwardly calm and peaceful. It was only among the black population that discontent and rebellion prevailed.

For Nat Turner these years of quiet were climaxed in 1825. The young man commanded the respect of all who knew him, and even his master stood in awe of him. However, that year, when he was placed under a new overseer, the seeds of trouble were sown.

Of all those involved in the slave system, the overseers were the worst. They were poor white men, working for wages and hired by slaveowners to get as much work as possible out of the slaves by whatever means they could. They hated and feared the black people and were ruthless in their treatment of them, sometimes even beating a slave to death.

Nat's new overseer was one of these, and it was not long before a quarrel broke out between the two. Unwilling to bow before this white man, Nat Turner ran away. Strong and clever enough not to be caught, he made for the woods, where he could hide in safety, and for thirty days he enjoyed the liberty of a free man.

Turner never had much to say about those thirty days. He was free to escape to the North, as his father had done. The thought must have intoxicated him. But he was alone. His freedom was a personal freedom. What of his black brothers, the slaves who looked to him for leadership? What of his divine mission? "The Spirit appeared to me," he said later, "and said I had my wishes directed to the things of this world and not to the kingdom of Heaven, and that I should return." And so he did—freely, he returned to slavery!

The blacks on the plantation were astonished to see him again. They thought surely by that time he had made his way to some other part of the country. They found fault with him, saying he must be crazy to have come back. They said that if they were in his place they would not serve any master in the world. The freedom-loving slaves were angry and suspicious of a man who would willingly return to slavery, and their confidence in Nat was shaken.

But Nat Turner knew what he was doing. There in the woods the power of belief, the power of righteous anger, the power of blackness met in his soul. For he had seen a vision—"and I saw white spirits and black spirits engaged in a battle, and the sun was darkened—the thunder rolled in the Heavens, and the blood flowed in streams—and I heard a voice saying, 'Such is your luck, and such you are called to see, and let it come rough or smooth, you must surely bear it.'"

From that time on he became obsessed with the idea of black liberation. He knew that every slave was at heart a revolutionary and that, no matter what the white slaveowners might say, every slave craved freedom. And he had at hand a revolutionary doctrine that fit his purpose perfectly—the Christian religion.

Nat Turner became a preacher. He was not a regularly ordained minister or an enrolled member of any church, but he gathered his followers together in secret each Sunday and spoke to them of Christ and of his own mystic experiences.

There are things about this fanatical black mystic that will forever remain a mystery. His fierce religious spirit produced in him an odd mixture of gentleness, ruthlessness, and piety, so that he emerges as one of the most fascinating rebels in American history.

Very little is known of Nat Turner's wife. She was a slave woman living on another plantation under another master, and the young couple could meet only in secret. It was impossible for Turner to give his wife the protection of a husband or to be a true father to his son, Redic. With his great pride in his black manhood, the situation enraged him. Yet under the slave system even a man of Turner's stature was helpless. In trying to explain Turner's motives in revolting, the tragic fact of his family life is often used. Surely this gave him additional cause to hate slavery and the plantation system.

Turner knew that if he was ever to strike a blow against the hated system, he must organize the people. His preaching gave him a chance to do this. Secretly, slaves would come from miles around to meet and listen to his fiery sermons. His fame as a preacher reached the ears of the white men. One of these, Etheldred T. Brantley, attended Turner's meetings and was so impressed by his teaching that he reformed his life and asked to be baptized by the black man. Since the white people would not let the baptism take place in their church, Turner and Brantley went down to the river and were baptized together. "After this," Turner said later, "I rejoiced greatly and gave thanks to God."

On May 12, 1828, Nat had another vision. "I heard a

loud voice in the heavens, and the Spirit instantly appeared to me and said that . . . the time was fast approaching when the first should be last and the last
should be first," he explained later. He said the spirit
told him he should wait for a sign from heaven, and then
he should begin his great work. "I should arise and
prepare myself, and slay my enemies with their own
weapons." Meanwhile he must wait. Wait for a sign!
To a man of Nat's passionate nature, these restraining
thoughts were hard to accept.

In Boston David Walker saw no need to wait. In that
year of 1828 he had already begun to agitate. A free
black, Walker was born in Wilmington, North Carolina.
When he was about thirty years old, he moved North,
carrying with him a great hatred of slavery. He became
active in Boston's Colored Association, and in 1829 he
wrote his famous *Appeal,* calling on the slaves to rise
up against their enslavers.

"Are we men?" he wrote. "I ask you, are we men?"
He quoted the Declaration of Independence to show
that the blacks had a right to use force in resisting the
oppression of white masters. "They want us for their
slaves," he continued, "and think nothing of murdering
us in order to subject us to that wretched condition—
therefore, if there is an attempt made by us, kill or be
killed. . . ."

The plan to ship more black Americans to Liberia was
bitterly opposed by Walker. "Let no man of us budge
one step," he wrote. "America is more our country than
it is the whites'—we have enriched it with our blood and
tears. The greatest riches in all America have arisen
from our blood and tears."

Walker's *Appeal* caused great excitement throughout the country, especially in the slave South. Steps were taken to keep the publication from falling into the hands of the slaves, but Walker and his friends devoted all their time to the distribution and reprinting of the stirring text. In 1830 the pamphlet went into a third edition. That same year David Walker died mysteriously.

The slaves were quick to react to Walker's *Appeal*. All over the South fires broke out, the work of black men striking against their enslavers. Uprisings were plotted in a half dozen Southern states.

Thoughtful white men realized what was happening. "The slaves are men," one wrote. "They have within them that inextinguishable thirst for freedom which is born in man. They are already writhing in their shackles. They will, one day, throw them off with vindictive violence, if we do not unloose them."

By the beginning of 1830 Nat Turner was "writhing in his shackles," longing for the day when he would rise up and "slay the enemy with their own weapons." It was at this time that he began working for Joseph Travis. His former master, Putnam Moore, had died, and late in 1829 his widow, Sarah Moore, married Travis, taking her slaves with her to her new home.

Travis had great confidence in Nat, and some claim that he gave him the position of foreman. Turner himself said that he had no reason to complain of the treatment he received from Travis. White Southerners were amazed that he should revolt against such a "kind master." They failed to see the viewpoint of a revolutionary slave: A "kind slavemaster" was a contradiction in terms.

Like all great leaders, Nat Turner was able to sense the mood and feelings of his people, not only in the county where he lived but throughout the country. He was aware that for several years the whole black population had been stirring with discontent and protest. It is possible, even probable, that he had read David Walker's fervent *Appeal*. It is certain that he shared Walker's convictions.

Moreover, Turner knew that there were almost 1,800 free blacks in Southampton County alone. These men were a constant inspiration to the slaves. Since they knew what it was to be free, they could probably be counted on to help in a move toward freedom. As for the slaves themselves, their whole lives centered around the urge to resist. Turner was sure that every slave had the makings of a revolutionary. In these thoughts he may have been naïve.

In February, 1831, there was an eclipse of the sun. Turner, searching eagerly for a sign from his God, decided this was what he had been waiting for. Now he felt free to go ahead with his plans. He called together his four most trusted followers—Henry Porter, Hark Travis, Nelson Williams, and Samuel Francis. All were eager to join him in a strike for freedom. The plot was simple and clear. The small band of men would begin at the nearby plantations. As they moved from one to the other, the slaves who had been prepared by Turner's preaching would join them in the fighting. The Fourth of July was set as the day of the uprising.

Turner was ill on July 4, and the campaign had to be postponed. The band of revolutionaries waited for another sign. This came to them on Saturday, August 13—

"a greenish-blue color of the sun." The next day was Sunday. The slaves gathered at a religious meeting in the southern part of the county, and Turner spoke to them. His supporters showed their willingness to follow him by wearing red bandanas around their necks.

A week later, on Sunday, August 21, the leaders of the rebellion met in the woods near the Travis estate. The night before Nat had instructed Henry and Hark to prepare a dinner for the group. Hark brought a pig and Henry brought brandy, and they cooked the food there in the woods. Two more slaves, Will and Jack, had joined them.

Turner was not with the men for dinner but waited until afternoon before making his appearance. Seeing the two new men, he questioned them. Jack was well known to him as a good friend of Hark Travis'. Will was said to be the strongest man in the county. Six feet tall and well built, he was the slave of a very cruel master. His back was covered with scars from countless whippings. He hated his master so much that he refused to adopt his last name and was known simply as Will. His hatred was well founded. The master had sold Will's wife to a slave trader, and she was lost to him forever.

Seeing Will among his followers on that Sunday afternoon, Turner asked him how he came to be there. Will replied that his life was not as precious to him as his liberty. "And do you hope to gain your liberty?" Nat asked. Will answered that he would gain it or lose his life in the attempt.

Turner was satisfied. "This was enough," he said, "to put [me] in full confidence." He began immediately to outline the plan of attack. They would strike that night, beginning with the Travis home and proceeding from house to house. As they went they would be joined by other slaves from the various houses. They would also take whatever arms and horses they could find. With these they would proceed to Jerusalem, which was the county seat of Southampton. In Jerusalem they expected to find arms and ammunition enough to continue their struggle, but until they did their chief weapons must be speed and secrecy.

Turner gave orders to his men that no white person was to be left alive during the first attacks. In this way he hoped to strike terror and alarm among his enemies. Later women and children would be spared, along with any men who did not resist. Looting and rape were to have no part in the advance. "Remember that ours is not a war for robbery nor to satisfy our passions," he told his men. "It is a struggle for freedom. Ours must be deeds, not words."

About ten o'clock that night all was ready, and the little band of seven men set out on their crusade against slavery. It was Turner himself who struck the first blow. At the Travis plantation, Turner's master and all his family were killed. The rebels took what arms they could find, as well as horses, and then pushed on to the next house. Everywhere slaves flocked to join them. Within twenty-four hours the original band of seven had become more than seventy.

As the numbers of his army increased, Turner organized his striking force. "I took my station in the rear," he said later, "and as it was my object to carry terror and devastation wherever we went, I placed fifteen or twenty of the best armed and most to be relied on in the front, who generally approached the houses as fast as their horses could run; this was for two purposes— to prevent escape and strike terror into the inhabitants."

Turner's part in the raids was that of commanding officer. Armed only with a light sword, he left the actual killing to his followers and devoted his time to organizing and commanding his men. But he was determined that no white person should escape alive. At the Whitehead plantation, when a young white girl tried to run away from the scene of the fighting he chased after her. His sword was so dull that he could not kill her with that, so he picked up a fence rail and killed her with a blow on the head.

Riding behind his men, he usually got to the houses in time to see the work of death completed. "I viewed the mangled bodies as they lay, in silent satisfaction," he stated, "and immediately started in quest of other victims."

All through the night the black army moved forward, leaving death in its path. No one with a white skin was spared except one family that was too poor to own slaves. Within forty hours fifty-seven white people had been killed.

Monday morning, when the bodies were first discovered by the white people, terror gripped the countryside. A volunteer force was quickly organized among the neighboring planters and set out along the blood-stained track in pursuit of the rebel band.

Meanwhile Turner pushed on. After riding and fighting all Sunday night and Monday morning, he brought his forces together and started for Jerusalem. By now all his men were mounted and the little army could

move forward quickly. But just three miles from the
city they came to the gate of James Parker's estate.
Some of the men wanted to try to recruit more fighters
from among Parker's slaves, but Turner was opposed
to this. He was eager to reach Jerusalem as soon as possible. The men argued with him. Some had relatives at
Parker's house who would surely be glad to join them.
Finally Turner gave in and agreed to let the men go
up to the house. It was a fatal mistake.

Turner waited with a handful of men there at the
Parker gate while the rest of the band went up to the
house, which lay across the field about a half mile away.

Parker and his family were not there when the black
men reached the house. The men were all tired from
the long hours of fighting and decided to rest awhile
and drink some of the applejack from Parker's well-
stocked cellar. Nat became impatient with the delay.
Leaving seven or eight men at the gate, he set out for
the house to see what was keeping the others.

It was on this small group of men at Parker's gate
that the white volunteer army made its first counter-
attack. The blacks were outnumbered two to one and
were forced to retreat. At this moment Turner returned
with the rest of the men. Some of them were quite
drunk from the Parker applejack, but Turner took in the
situation immediately and formed his line of attack.

The white fighters retreated. Turner and his men
chased them over the fields and up the hill. But on the
other side of the hill they were met by a much larger
party of whites. These had come quickly out from
Jerusalem as soon as news of the revolt reached the
town.

Against this greater force the black band was power-less. For the most part, they were armed only with axes and clubs. In the first quick attacks, when the whites were taken by surprise, these arms had been very effective. But the few guns that the slaves had been able to gather were not really fit to use and were hope-lessly inadequate against the well-equipped militia. The rebels were forced to scatter and take cover.

Several of Turner's bravest men were wounded in the struggle. Will was killed. During the raids Will had fought so fiercely that Nat had nicknamed him the Ex-ecutioner. His only weapon was a broad ax, sharp and heavy. Revenge, as well as a longing for freedom, filled his heart, and he struck out brutally against his enemies. When he fell, it was with his broad ax lifted, ready to strike. According to one story, his last words were, "Bury my ax with me."

Hark had his horse shot from under him, but Nat caught him another that had lost its rider, and together the two took off into the woods. They were joined by about twenty men. All the rest had scattered or been captured. Knowing that an attack on Jerusalem was im-possible with such a small force, Turner had to be con-tent with a few quick raids against the enemy. He still hoped to gather his men together again, find new re-cruits, and carry on.

But the battle at Parker's field had been the turning point. By the morning of the twenty-fourth, the full force of the slave state's military organization had been called up. Three companies of artillery rushed to the scene. Two warships at anchor in a nearby harbor sent detachments of fighting men. These were joined by hundreds of soldiers from volunteer and militia companies throughout Virginia and North Carolina. In all about 3,000 armed men came to Southampton to put down the revolt.

If Nat Turner had succeeded in entering Jerusalem and capturing its arms and ammunition, he might have kept fighting for many days. Properly armed, his black army could have moved into the Great Dismal Swamp, which extended from Southampton County into North Carolina, and from this strategic point the blacks could have waged effective guerrilla warfare. As it was, the little band of black men was forced to break up. Turner found himself alone, except for Nat Reese and Jacob Charlton. He sent them out to look for his friends Henry, Sam, Nelson, and Hark, with instructions to meet him in the woods where the leaders had had their dinner the Sunday before. But when Turner reached the place he found himself surrounded by a white search party. His men were not able to join him, and he was forced to give up all hope for the present and go into hiding.

The quick defeat of the revolt was the result of several things: the poor arms and lack of ammunition of the blacks, the fact that some of them became drunk, the separation of the forces that took place against Turner's will at the Parker gate, and finally, the greater force and arms of the whites.

During the fighting forty-eight blacks were taken prisoner by the troops from Jerusalem. In the days that followed many more were massacred. Black men were killed on sight. They were cut down with barbarity and without trial. One newspaper account stated, "Men were tortured to death, burned, maimed and subjected to nameless atrocities. The overseers were called upon to point out any slaves whom they distrusted, and if any tried to escape they were cut down." Another report said, "Many Negroes are killed every day. The exact number will never be known." But it is known that over 100 blacks were murdered in Southampton County alone—at least twice as many as the number of white people who had fallen at the hands of the slaves.

Panic flashed through Virginia. One man wrote, "Every white man in this place is scared to death." A woman wrote, "Our whites unhappily show too much fear of those wretches. It is like a smothered volcano— we know not when or where the flames will burst forth, but we know that death in the most horrid form threatens us."

The panic spread from Virginia, up to Delaware and down to Florida, across to Louisiana, and up again to Kentucky. The lid which the slave states had clamped down on the press was blown off. News of Nat Turner's revolt was published throughout the South. The slaves, who had already been restless, followed Turner into rebellion.

In September a rumor spread that 2,000 blacks were hiding in the Great Dismal Swamp. The whole military power of Virginia was pressed into service. Civilians were herded into forts and blockhouses. Maryland whites were also panic-stricken, and slaves in that state were arrested by the dozens. Terror was so great that at least three white men died of heart failure.

By October arrests were being made in Alabama, where a revolt of the slaves was feared. Two slaves were executed in South Carolina for plotting to revolt.

That same month six slaves were arrested in Georgia for conspiracy, and four of them were executed. In Tennessee the slaves plotted to set fire to some buildings and amid the confusion to seize as many guns as they could and start a general massacre. The plotters were "slashed with all severity."

Terror reigned for a full year after the Turner revolt. One important result of this was a series of laws passed by the slave states. Laws against free blacks, as well as against slaves, were already in effect throughout the South. Now these were increased. Free blacks were forbidden to meet in groups larger than twelve men, no free black was allowed to carry arms, and neither slaves nor free blacks were permitted to have religious services except with whites.

On the other hand, the Turner revolt had succeeded in opening up the question of slavery to public debate. Although the claim that the Virginia legislature came close to abolishing slavery in that state is not true, the issue was now out in the open. In the North abolition societies sprang up by the hundreds. White men, as well as blacks, began to speak and write about the evils of the slave system. One of the most outspoken was William Lloyd Garrison, who wrote, "Insurrections are the natural and consequent productions of slavery—experience has proved this in all ages and in all nations where slavery has existed. Slavery ought to be, must be, and shall be abolished in these United States."

The important moral and social issues involved could no longer be ignored. Sides were taken throughout the country—two opposing ways of life met and clashed. The line between "slavocracy" and democracy was

clearly drawn. In its Two Hundred Years' War against
slavery, the black army was at last gaining valuable
white allies.

While all these great forces stormed around them,
the small band of black revolutionaries faced death in
Southampton County, Virginia. Their leader and prophet
was still in hiding. Against the might of their white
captors they had no defense. They had used violence to
oppose the violence of the slave system. They were condemned. Sixteen slaves and three free blacks were executed within a few weeks of the uprising. Among them
were Turner's closest friends, Hark Travis, Samuel
Francis, and Nelson Williams.

As so often happened, it was left to the white report-
ers to praise their courage. "All died bravely," one
wrote, "indicating no reluctance to lose their lives in
such a cause." Another said, "Some of them that were
wounded and in the agonies of death declared that they
were going happy, for God had a hand in what they had
been doing." Their leader had taught them to value liberty more than life.

In those days of terror even Turner's wife was made
to suffer. She was tortured under the lash to try to make
her produce her husband's papers.

But what of Nat Turner himself? Rumors about him
were everywhere. Some said he had been caught, some
that he had run away into Maryland, some that he had
been drowned. The governor of Virginia offered a $500
reward for his capture and issued the following description: "Nat is between 30 and 35 years old [he was just
thirty-one], 5 feet 6 or 8 inches high, weighs between
150 and 160 pounds, rather bright complexion, but not

a mulatto, broad shoulders, large flat nose, large eyes, broad flat feet, rather knock-kneed, walks brisk and active, hair on top of the head very thin, no beard except on the upper lip and the top of the chin, a scar on one of his temples, also one on the back of his neck, a large knot on one of his bones of the right arm, near the wrist, produced by a blow." The whole countryside was on the alert for this man.

When his friends failed to join him, Turner went into hiding where he was, on the Travis estate. He scratched out a hole under a pile of fence rails in a field and hid there for six weeks. All day long, while his enemies searched the countryside, he lay in hiding. He had supplied himself with food taken from the Travis house. Only in the dead of night did he go outside and then just for a few minutes to get water from a nearby brook.

As the weeks passed and he was still free he started to go about at night to see what he could learn at the houses in the neighborhood. But he was afraid to speak to anyone and returned each morning to his cave. One night while he was out a dog entered his cave, attracted by some meat he had there. Turner met the dog just as he was returning in the morning. A few nights later the same dog came back again with two black men. This time the dog found Turner and started to bark. Seeing the fugitive in the woods, the two men became frightened and ran, but Turner realized that he was no longer safe in his hiding place. For two weeks he moved from place to place.

"During the time I was pursued, I had many hairbreadth escapes," Nat stated later. "I was taken a fort-

night afterwards by Mr. Benjamin Phipps, in a little hole
I had dug out with my sword, for the purpose of con-
cealment, under the top of a fallen tree. On Mr. Phipps'
discovering the place, he cocked his gun and aimed at
me. I requested him not to shoot and I would give up,
upon which he demanded my sword. I delivered it to
him, and he brought me to prison." He knew that it was
impossible to escape because the woods were full of
men hunting him. He thought it best to surrender then
and try to escape later. It was October 30, and he had
been a fugitive for more than two months.

The mysterious black leader, the "great bandit," was
now in the hands of his enemies, who viewed him with
terror and curiosity. How had he performed this terrible
deed—and why? A lawyer named Thomas R. Gray
was chosen by the court to find the answers. He visited
Turner in prison and talked to him. On the basis of their
talks, Gray wrote an account of the uprising and of Turner's former life, which was published as *The Confes-
sions of Nat Turner*. A few years ago a fictionalized ver-
sion of Turner's life was published by William Styron
under the same title. Gray's work remains the main
source of information on the black leader and his deeds.

Gray was impressed by Turner. "He is a complete fa-
natic, or plays his part most admirably," he wrote. "On
other subjects he possesses an uncommon share of intelligence, with a mind capable of attaining anything. He
is below the ordinary stature, though strong and active,
having the true Negro face, every feature of which is
strongly marked. . . .

"The calm, deliberate composure with which he spoke

of his late deeds and intentions, the expression of his fiend-like face when excited by enthusiasm, still bearing the stains of the blood of helpless innocence about him; clothed with rags and covered with chains; yet daring to raise his manacled hands to heaven, with a spirit soaring above the attributes of man; I looked on him and my blood curdled in my veins."

Nat Turner's plans were defeated, his followers destroyed, and yet he had not failed. He had furthered the idea and cause of freedom because he had chosen to act for freedom.

Saturday, November 5, 1831, Nat Turner was brought to trial in the county court at Jerusalem. His "confession," in which he freely told of his part in the revolt, was read before the court. But Turner pleaded not guilty. He explained to the court that he did not feel guilty.

Can a man commit a crime against slavery?

The prisoner produced no evidence other than his written confession and the case was submitted to the six judges of the court, who quickly declared him guilty. Jeremiah Cobb pronounced the sentence: "The judgment of the court is that you be taken hence to the jail from whence you came, thence to the place of execution, and on Friday next, between the hours of 10 A.M. and 2 P.M. be hung by the neck until you are dead! dead! dead! and may the Lord have mercy on your soul."

He went calmly to his death. He looked back without regret. He looked forward in hope that his sacrifice would bear fruit in the longed-for black resurrection. His mission was completed.

Judge Cobb had repeated the sentence three times—

dead! dead! dead!—but at the moment of his execution, Nat Turner had only begun to live.

"Do you not find yourself mistaken now?" Gray had asked him.

Nat answered, "Was not Christ crucified?"

Part III
Frederick Douglass and the Crisis

7

The Making of an Abolitionist

The year 1831 marked a turning point in the black man's struggle against slavery. For many years the conscience of America had been dulled to the great evil that blighted the nation's life. While the free states contended against the slave states over the expansion of slavery into new territory, the issue was one of sectional power and was chiefly political in nature.

Two events were responsible for the change. In Virginia Nat Turner rose up, the avenger of his black brothers, the prophet of things to come, a martyr to the cause of freedom. With one desperate act, he flashed across the scene of American life leaving a lasting impression. Some loved him, many feared and hated him, but no one could forget him. The sword he carried into battle split the country in two. Over the next thirty years, the two camps would drift farther and farther apart, heading for the final rupture of the Civil War.

Even earlier in 1831 another weapon was raised against the slave system. The *Liberator* was published in Boston, Massachusetts. Printed on borrowed paper with a borrowed press, this newspaper denounced slavery as the greatest evil under the sun. Its editor, a twenty-six-year-old white man named William Lloyd Garrison, took his stand in that first edition. He called for the immediate emancipation of the slaves. "I am in earnest," he wrote, "I will not retreat a single inch— and I WILL BE HEARD."

As other abolitionists joined their voices to that of Garrison, the burden of the battle for freedom shifted from the slave to his newly acquired allies. Until the Civil War slaves continued to rise up in rebellion against their enslavers. Like Nat Turner, they used whatever weapons they could lay their hands on—stolen guns, homemade swords and bayonets. But against the armed might of the slave system these had little effect.

Another event occurred in 1831 that seemed unimportant at the time: after years of effort, a fourteen-year-old slave named Frederick Augustus Washington Bailey learned to read. Later he would change his name to Frederick Douglass, but in 1831 he found the weapon he would use to influence the destiny of his black brothers. His weapon was words.

Like many slaves, young Frederick knew little about his own birth. He never knew who his own father was or what day and year he was born. There was a rumor that his master was his father, but Harriet Bailey died without telling her son anything. From other events he was able to figure he was probably born in February, 1817.

Although Fred scarcely ever saw his mother, his earliest memories were happy. He lived with his grandparents on his master's Maryland plantation. His grandfather, Isaac Bailey, was a free man married to a slave. The old couple were allowed to live in a little hut owned by Frederick's master, where they were put in charge of the small black children who were still too young to be useful slaves.

Poor and miserable in many ways, the little home was a happy one, full of love and fun. But the freedom of those early years came to a sudden end when Fred was seven years old. It was one of the saddest days of his life when his grandmother took him through the woods to the house of his master, Captain Anthony, and left him there alone among strangers. The burden of slavery had fallen on his small shoulders.

Although Captain Anthony owned several slaves to take care of his house and gardens, he himself was the manager of a large plantation belonging to Colonel Lloyd. Fred, living in Anthony's own house, did not suffer as his fellow slaves did. His duties were light: driving the cows home in the evening, keeping the chickens out of the garden, and running errands. Yet his experiences on the Lloyd plantation roused in him a deep hatred of slavery. Years later he used these experiences to awaken others to the brutality and injustice of the system.

Free to roam over the plantation, the boy saw sights and heard stories that filled him with rage. He was struck by the contrast between the way Lloyd lived and the condition of his slaves. Nothing was too fine for the big house on the hill and for the white family that lived there, but the slaves were not even given enough to eat. They had nothing except the bare necessities of life. Their weekly supply of food did not keep them from going hungry, and their yearly supply of clothes did not keep them warm. At night they slept on the floor.

In spite of this the slaves were expected to work from dawn until night, six days a week, winter and summer. When they rebelled against such treatment, the overseer's whip made them submit. Any black who did anything the overseer didn't like was beaten until his back was raw and bleeding. If he didn't get up on time, he was beaten. If he talked back, he was beaten. If he didn't answer when spoken to, he was beaten. If the overseer didn't like the way he looked or the way he walked or the way he stood, he was beaten.

Two instances of this inhuman treatment etched themselves on Fred's mind. His Aunt Hester, who was also a slave of Captain Anthony's, had been ordered to keep away from her young black lover who worked on the plantation. Hester disobeyed. Her enraged master stripped her to the waist and beat her with a cowhide whip until her blood ran to the floor. Fred, sleeping in a closet off the kitchen, was awakened by the sound of his master's oaths and the cries of his poor aunt. Seeing the horrible scene, he was terrified and crouched in the corner shivering with fear.

Even more cruel was the overseer of Lloyd's plantation, a man named Gore. One day Gore tried to beat a powerful young slave by the name of Bill Demby. Demby rebelled. He broke away and ran into a nearby brook, where he stood with the water up to his shoulders, refusing to come out. Gore told him that he would count to three, and that if Demby did not come out, he would be shot. Demby stood his ground. At the count of three, Gore fired—and shot him dead. Blood stained the water red as Demby's body sank slowly from sight.

Gore tried to justify his act by saying that Demby's behavior was setting a bad example for the other slaves. His crime went unpunished.

Frederick himself was rarely beaten by his master, but he suffered from hunger and cold. The cold was particularly hard for the little boy to bear. All year long his only clothing was a shirt reaching to his knees—no shoes, no jacket or coat. He had no bed. "I used to steal a bag used for carrying corn to the mill," he remembered later. "I would crawl into this bag and sleep there on the cold damp clay floor with my head in and my feet out."

He was learning the brutal facts of slave life fast. One thing that impressed him greatly was the way the slaves sang. It seemed to him that all the bitter anguish of their souls went into those songs. White people mistakenly thought the slaves sang because they were happy. Nothing could be farther from the truth. They sang of resistance and rebellion. They sang to God for help in their struggle for freedom from their captors.

The more he saw, the more Fred hated slavery. Young as he was, he was overwhelmed by the thought that he was a slave forever. With all his heart he longed to be free.

When he was about nine years old, his first real break came and he took his first step on the long road that would lead to freedom. Lucretia Auld, Captain Anthony's married daughter, took an interest in the sturdy, bright-eyed little boy. Knowing that her father's slaves often went hungry, she gave Fred extra food whenever she had a chance. Fred became her pet and ran errands for her. One day Lucretia announced that she had arranged to send Fred to live with her brother-in-law and his family in Baltimore. Fred was overcome with joy. Scrubbed and combed, wearing his first pair of trousers, he set out for a new life in the city.

It was indeed a new life. "I was treated like a pig on the plantation," he remarked later; "I was treated as a child now."

Mr. and Mrs. Hugh Auld had never owned a slave. They received Fred into their home with an affection that he had never known before. Mrs. Auld was by nature a kind and gentle woman, and she treated Fred in much the same way as she did her own son, Tommy. It was Fred's duty to look after the little white boy, and he did it with pleasure. For the first time he developed a real affection for white people.

For all slaves, life in Baltimore was very different from plantation life. In spite of all the laws restricting their activities, they had privileges that were altogether unknown to their country cousins. Many were allowed to practice a trade, and although all their earnings became the property of their masters, they were well fed and clothed and even treated with a certain respect. The little boy from Maryland's eastern shore thrived on city life.

One of Fred's delights was to stand by his new mistress' side while she read aloud to him and little Tommy. One day he asked her to teach him to read. Not knowing it was against the law of Maryland to teach a slave to read, she agreed. Fred made such good progress in his lessons that Mrs. Auld proudly told her husband.

Mr. Auld flew into a rage. He said it was "unsafe" to teach a slave.

"If you give a nigger an inch," he said, "he will take a mile. Learning will spoil the best nigger in the world. He should know nothing but the will of his master and learn how to obey it. If you teach that nigger to read, it will forever unfit him for the duties of a slave. If he learns how to read, he'll want to know how to write. And then, he'll be running away with himself."

That ended the reading lessons. Mrs. Auld listened to her husband and obeyed him.

Fred listened too, and what he heard made him think. "Very well," he thought, "knowledge makes a child unfit to be a slave. Knowledge is the path that leads from slavery to freedom." He had already made up his mind that he did not want to be a slave. Now Mr. Auld had shown him the best way to work toward his own freedom.

By starting to teach Fred to read, Mrs. Auld had given him an "inch." Now, all by himself, he decided to take the "mile." But teaching himself to read was a hard job. He looked for help and found it among the white playmates whom he met on the streets of Baltimore. Each time he was sent on an errand he carried a book with him. When he met one of his friends, he would ask for a lesson in reading and spelling. His white friends were willing to teach him, especially since he carried apples and biscuits in his pockets to pay for his lessons. It was a long process, but at last the milestone was reached. He could read!

Fred's favorite book, bought with the pennies he had been able to save, was *The Columbia Orator*. It was a book of speeches denouncing slavery and praising justice. True, the speeches were made in behalf of Catholic emancipation in England, but the arguments rang with a universal truth. The young black boy read them over and over. Eagerly he read the accounts of Nat Turner's revolt in the Baltimore newspapers and listened as the white people discussed that terrible event. Many blamed the revolt on the *Liberator*, which had been published a few months before, but since only four copies of that first edition had managed to reach the South, it was impossible that the two events were directly connected.

It would be many years before Frederick read his first copy of Garrison's paper, but already the word "abolition" was on everyone's lips. The fourteen-year-old boy listened. He hunted out all the news he could about the abolitionist movement, but he never dreamed that he would one day be a leader in that cause.

His hatred of slavery grew. "Slaveholders," he thought, "are only a band of successful robbers who left their homes and went to Africa to steal my people and make them slaves." More than anything else, he wanted to be free.

His friends encouraged him in his hope for liberty. One old friend, a religious black man named Lawson, was convinced that the Lord had a great work for Fred to do. Fred was puzzled. "How can that be?" he asked. "I'm a slave and a slave forever."

Lawson replied, "If you want freedom, ask the Lord for it and He will give it to you."

Two of Fred's friends were Irishmen whom he met on the Baltimore docks. They said it was a pity that such a fine young fellow should be a slave and advised him to run away to the North, where he could be free.

Fred knew that he was still too young to run away, but he started planning for the day when he could make his escape. He was willing to pray to God for freedom, but he would work toward it too. How could he prepare? He decided to learn how to write.

When Fred reached his teens he began working for his master, who was a shipbuilder. As he was helping the carpenters on the ship, he noticed that each piece of timber was marked with a certain letter to indicate where it was to be used. Left alone to watch the shipyard while the others went to lunch, he spent his time copying these letters. This was the beginning. From his friends he learned how to write other letters, and he carried a piece of chalk around with him so he could practice writing on fences and pavements.

He didn't tell his mistress and master that he was learning to write, but when he was alone in the house he borrowed Tommy's school books and carefully copied the writing. At this time he was living in a little room over the kitchen. He carried a barrel and a chair up there, and when the rest of the family was asleep he sat at the barrel-top desk copying all the books he had. After many a weary hour, he finally succeeded in learning to write.

Although Fred continued to live with Mr. and Mrs. Hugh Auld, he remained the "property" of his old master, Captain Anthony. Upon Captain Anthony's death in 1830 it was necessary to have all his property evaluated so that it could be equally divided between his two heirs. The valuation was a bitter experience for

Fred. "We were all ranked together," he said, "men and women with horses, sheep and swine, all holding the same rank in the scale of being, all subject to the same narrow examination." After the valuation came the division. The fate of each slave was being decided for all his life, and he had no more voice in the decision than the animals.

By a lucky chance Frederick became the property of his old friend Lucretia Auld and was sent back to Baltimore again. But very soon after this Lucretia died, and he became the slave of her husband, Thomas Auld. Two years later, in 1832, Fred's good luck ran out. Thomas Auld married again and sent for him to come to work for him and his new wife.

Fred wished he had not delayed his plans to run away. Now it was too late. Sadly he made the trip back to Maryland's eastern shore, where his new master had a farm near the village of St. Michaels.

After his life in the city, Fred found work as a field hand awful. Once again he learned what it was to be hungry. In fact, he and the other slaves on the Auld plantation were half starved.

Fred had no respect for his new master. He was even worse than most slaveowners, being both cruel and cowardly. Oddly enough, he claimed to be a religious man. When he whipped one of his slaves he would quote the Bible, saying, "He that knoweth his master's will and doeth it not shall be beaten with many stripes." This attempt to use religion to justify slavery enraged Frederick, who knew the Bible taught that all men were free and equal in the sight of God, their only true master.

Frederick refused to submit himself to Thomas Auld, and the two were constantly at odds with one another. Finally Auld declared that he was completely unmanageable and would have to be broken.

Not far from St. Michaels lived a man named Edward Covey, who was well known as a first-rate hand at breaking young blacks. He was a poor white man who rented his farmland and needed cheap labor to help him work it. When a slaveholder had an unruly slave he would hire him out to Covey for a small sum of money, and in return Covey would see to it that the slave was broken. He would treat the slave with such extreme cruelty and work him so hard that his spirit would be completely crushed. With this treatment in mind, Auld rented Fred to Covey for a period of one year. He was about seventeen at that time.

Now started the worst months of Fred's life. Covey beat him mercilessly with sticks and cowhide whips until his shoulders were covered with open sores. The rough quality of his clothes prevented the sores from healing, and since the whippings were repeated each week, his back was constantly raw and bleeding. Unlike Thomas Auld, Covey gave his slaves enough food to eat, but he worked them so hard they never had time enough to eat it.

"Work, work, work," Frederick Douglass wrote later of these months. "It was never too hot or too cold; it could never rain, blow, snow or hail too hard for us to work in the fields. At certain seasons we were all kept in the fields until eleven or twelve o'clock at night. Mr. Covey succeeded in breaking me—in body, soul and spirit. My natural elasticity was crushed; my intellect languished; the disposition to read departed; the cheerful spark in my eye died out; the dark night of slavery closed in upon me, and behold a man transformed to a brute!"

One hot August day Fred was working with three other men on Covey's farm treading the wheat. This required that all four of them work together, so even though Fred was feeling sick, he kept on working. Finally it became too much for him, and he fell to the ground. When Covey saw him lying there he kicked him and ordered him to get up and go back to work. Several times Fred tried to rise, but he was not able. So Covey took a very heavy stick and hit him over the head, saying, "If you have got a headache, I'll cure you." Then, leaving him with his head bleeding, he returned to his work.

When Fred was able to rise he made up his mind to go to Thomas Auld, his owner, and explain the inhuman treatment he was receiving at Covey's farm. He felt that if Auld would not protect him out of human sympathy he would do it rather than see his own "property" so badly treated. So he went slowly and painfully through the woods to St. Michaels.

At first Auld was deeply affected by what he saw and heard, but then he became hard and cold. He said, "If you should leave Covey now, I will lose your wages for the whole year. You must go back to him, come what may."

So Fred dragged himself wearily back through the woods to Covey's farm. On his return, Covey greeted him quite pleasantly, but the next morning when they met in the barn Covey attacked the youth and tried to whip him. Suddenly Fred decided to stand up for himself. He hit Covey hard. Now they were no longer master and slave; they were two men matched in a fight. For two hours they fought. Covey, knowing that he could not beat Fred in a fair fight, called to the other farm workers to help him. They refused. At last Covey gave up. He was beaten.

From that time on Covey never laid a hand on Fred. If he had turned him over to the authorities, Fred probably would have died, since it was the law in Maryland that a slave could be hanged for resisting his master. But Covey did nothing. Fred guessed it was because he would lose his reputation as a slave breaker if people learned that he had been beaten by a slave.

As for Fred, this fight was the turning point in his life as a slave. He wrote, "I was a changed being after the fight. I was nothing before; I was A MAN NOW." All his self-respect and self-confidence returned. He had reached the point where he was not afraid to die. This spirit made him a free man in fact, although he was still a slave by law.

At the end of the year Fred was again hired out by his master, this time to William Freeland. Freeland was a good man who treated his slaves well. Fred had grown large and strong and was proud of the fact that he could do as much work as any of the older men. Freeland held each slave responsible for his own conduct so that, though Fred worked hard, he enjoyed more leisure than he had since his days in Baltimore.

With leisure came thoughts of his fellow slaves. Frederick longed to help them and share his knowledge with them. He organized a small school which met secretly in the woods each Sunday. About forty young men defied the law and risked their safety to meet him there, and most of them were rewarded by learning how to read.

As Fred grew older he became ashamed to be content with his bondage. He had been thinking and speaking of freedom for years, and in January, 1836, he decided to make a break for it. From among his friends he chose five young men and told them his plan. He was the youngest of the group but took his place as their leader quite naturally. Although the others all wanted to be free, none had seriously thought of running away until Fred talked to them. The small group met at night to make their plans.

To run away! Since the first slaves came to the American shores, thousands of blacks had dreamed and planned and risked their lives to run away from their enslavers. But until recent years they had done it completely on their own; in their flight for freedom every white man was an enemy. The abolitionist movement changed all that. One of its greatest achievements was the establishment of the Underground Railroad, organized to help slaves escape from bondage.

This remarkable organization had stations reaching all the way from the deep South through the free states to Canada. Black men were transferred from one station to another, finding food and a bed in the abolitionists' own homes. They were guided through the woods at night, driven through the countryside concealed in farm wagons or hiding behind Quaker bonnets in some Quaker's carriage. Many were smuggled to liberty by sea. Pursuit by the slaveowners was always hot and ruthless.

They had the law on their side, and anyone willing to help a fugitive risked his own safety. Yet 3,200 volunteers staffed the railroad.

Among these the Quakers were outstanding. Levi Coffin, a Quaker from Cincinnati, was the "president" of the railroad and in his long career was personally responsible for the escape of 3,000 slaves. Calvin Fairbanks, Thomas Garrett, and John Fairfield were among the most daring agents and conductors. The latter traveled through the South pretending to be a buyer and seller of blacks while, in fact, he was their rescuer. On one occasion he led twenty-eight slaves to safety by organizing them into a funeral procession.

If the white agents of the railroad risked much, the black workers risked far more. They knew that if they were caught they could expect no mercy at the hands of the Southern lawmakers. Yet hundreds of free blacks willingly risked their lives to help their brothers escape. David Ruggles, William Sill, and John Parker are among the better known.

"Follow the North Star." Any slave who was able to escape the watchful eyes of his overseer would hide in the woods until dark. Then, guided by the North Star, he would set out for the nearest Underground Railroad station. Thousands escaped on this famous route and lived to tell of the horrors of slavery to the people of the North.

Frederick and his friends knew that they could count on the railroad for help once they had succeeded in reaching one of its stations. They studied the map, trying to find the best route to the North. Chesapeake Bay lay before them, and escape by water seemed safer than escape by land. They planned to steal a canoe and paddle north to the head of the bay. Once land was reached they would turn the canoe adrift and go on by land until they reached a free state. The plan involved great risks, but they were determined to try.

Easter was coming. Some slaveowners gave their slaves permission to visit friends and relatives during the Easter holidays. So Frederick wrote out six passes, one for each man: "This is to certify that I, the undersigned, have given the bearer, my servant, full liberty to go to Baltimore to spend the Easter Holidays." He signed these with Mr. Freeland's initials. The men were not headed for Baltimore, but they hoped these passes might help if their journey was questioned.

At the last moment one of the six, Sandy Jenkins, decided not to go. The rest stood firm. Then, on the very morning they planned to leave a group of white men arrived at Mr. Freeland's house on horseback. Someone, perhaps Sandy, had given the plan away. The men were constables armed with guns, and when Frederick stepped forward to ask what they wanted they tied him up.

One of the others, Henry Harris, refused to be tied. He said, "Shoot me! You can't kill me but once. Shoot! and be damned. I won't be tied." And with pistols at his breast, he struck one of the men. All the constables joined in the fight, and Henry was soon beaten and tied.

As the men were carried off to jail, everyone they met seemed to be against them. All knew that Frederick was the leader, and they called out, "He ought to be hanged. He ought to be burned." But there was little evidence against them. Frederick spoke out saying that they had not actually run away. They had been quietly at work when they were taken. Where was the evidence against them?

After a few days in jail the other four men were released and returned to their masters. Only Frederick was left in jail. As the days went by he began to despair. He was afraid he would be sold to a slave trader and sent to Georgia or Alabama, where escape would be next to impossible and life as a slave would be misery.

Once again luck was with him. After a week of uncertainty his master, Thomas Auld, came for him. He told Frederick that he wanted him to go back to Baltimore to learn a trade and that if he behaved himself properly, he would be freed when he was twenty-five! It seemed too good to be true.

So, after four years in the country working in the fields, Frederick returned to Baltimore and the home of Hugh Auld. He went to work in the shipyard and within a few months he became an expert caulker, earning as much as any of the caulkers of Baltimore. He made many friends among the free blacks of the city and was invited to join their organization, the East Baltimore Mental Improvement Society. There he met Anna Murray, a free black working as a housekeeper for a wealthy family. They soon became engaged.

The free blacks of Baltimore took an active interest in the affairs of the day. As the abolitionist movement grew, their own lives became more difficult. Successful and law-abiding free blacks were a living argument against keeping the rest of the race enslaved, and laws were passed making it extremely difficult for a master to free his slaves or for a free black to make a living.

The slaveowners of the South had no intention of allowing the abolitionists to disturb their way of life. They did all they could to prevent these men from entering their states and to suppress free speech on the slavery issue. To a certain extent they succeeded. In 1836, at the insistence of the Southern delegates, the United States Congress passed a "gag rule" requiring that all petitions relating to slavery in any way should be permanently shelved.

The rights of free speech and a free press, the right of a citizen to travel freely within the United States, even the right of elected delegates to discuss issues of national importance—all were swept aside. Injustice led to more injustice, and the freedom of all Americans was threatened.

Many American citizens realized that the antislavery struggle was indeed a battle for their own democratic rights. Writing to Gerrit Smith in 1835, James G. Birney summed up the situation: "It has become absolutely necessary that slavery should cease in order that freedom may be preserved in any portion of the land."

After President Andrew Jackson retired to private life in 1837, it was in the Congress that the political giants of the day held forth. John C. Calhoun of South Carolina, leader of the Democratic Party, became the champion of the proslavery cause. He claimed that no society could prosper unless one part of the community lived off the labors of others. Henry Clay, the powerful leader of the Whig Party, also opposed the abolitionists. John Quincy Adams, former President of the United States, agreed with Clay on the abolition issue, but the

gag rule shocked him. As a member of the House of
Representatives he worked tirelessly for its repeal.
Session after session he fought for the right of petition.
Every effort short of physical violence was made to
silence him.

John Quincy Adams would not be silenced. Neither
would the abolitionists. The past years had seen a rapid
growth in their numbers. There were now more than
500 antislavery societies in the Northern states with a
membership of almost 150,000. Everywhere they met
with persecution and attack, and yet their numbers
grew. They seemed to thrive on opposition. Southern
states used every means in their power to keep the agi-
tators out, while in the North they became the victims
of angry mobs. Speakers were bombarded with rotten
eggs; their voices were drowned out by horns and
drums. Antislavery presses were thrown into the river;
abolitionist halls were burned to the ground. Yet with
each incident the movement grew.

Free blacks matched the work of whites. James Forten, a wealthy black manufacturer from Philadelphia,
came to the aid of William Lloyd Garrison with financial
support. Charles Lenox Remond and William C. Nell
toured the free states as agents of the American Anti-
Slavery Society. William P. Powell and Theodore Wright
worked hand-in-hand with Garrison.

How could a young man of Frederick's intellectual
gifts remain a slave in times like these? His master had
promised him his freedom at the age of twenty-five, but
would he keep his promise? Fred's work as a caulker
earned him a good wage, but as a slave he was obliged
to turn all his money over to Hugh Auld. After a few

months in Baltimore his longing for freedom once more stirred him to action. Once again he began to make plans for escape to the North.

This time there would be no escape under cover of night. He planned to travel openly by train, but he would need the proper papers. No free black could travel anywhere in the South without his free papers giving his name and detailed description. No slave could travel without a pass signed by his master. But a slave might borrow the papers of a free friend and use these to get to the North. It was a dangerous practice, since if any free black was caught without his papers he was in serious trouble. Yet many free blacks were willing to take the risk of lending their papers to help out their friends.

Frederick's friends would have gladly loaned him their papers, but none of the descriptions fit him at all. However, one friend had a sailor's protection paper with an American eagle at the top. It looked official, and Frederick hoped that the description would go unnoticed.

So, in September, 1838, Frederick boarded a train for Philadelphia armed with this paper and seventeen dollars, which Anna had given him. He was dressed as a sailor and had enough knowledge of ships and docks to be able to talk like one, but his heart was pounding. Soon the conductor entered the Negro car to collect tickets and examine the papers of the black passengers. He came to Frederick and said, "I suppose you have your free papers?"

"No, sir," Frederick replied, "I never carry my free papers to sea with me."

"But you have something to show that you are free, haven't you?"

"Yes, sir," he answered. "I have a paper with the American eagle on it, and that will carry me around the world."

The conductor glanced at the paper Frederick showed him and went on about his business. If he had stopped to examine the paper, Frederick would surely have been caught. Once more, luck was with him.

But the danger was not yet passed. At Wilmington, Delaware, he had to leave the train and take a steamboat to Philadelphia. Here the risk of arrest was very great, but he reached the boat safely and was soon on his way. From Philadelphia he took another train to New York. The whole trip took less than twenty-four hours, but in that time he had made the long journey from slavery to freedom.

Frederick walked the streets of New York, dazzled by all he saw. A new world seemed to be opening up before him. "I felt as one might feel upon escape from a den of hungry lions," he wrote to a friend. He was a free man, and his heart was filled with joy and expectation.

But soon the reality of his situation struck him. He was without a home, without friends, without work, without money, not knowing where he could turn for help. He looked on every white man he saw as an enemy, and among the black men he did not know whom he could trust. He spent what money he had for food and slept in a lumberyard.

At last he met a sailor who looked like a man he could trust. Always a good judge of character, Frederick

had chosen well this time. On hearing his story, the
sailor took him to David Ruggles, a black agent in the
Underground Railroad.

Now he was truly among friends. He spent the next
few days at the Ruggles' home and sent a letter to Anna
telling her to join him in New York. As soon as she arrived they were married in a ceremony performed by
the Rev. J. W. C. Pennington, himself a runaway slave
from Maryland.

David Ruggles offered advice as well as shelter. He
suggested that the young couple go to New Bedford,
Massachusetts, where Frederick might be able to find
work as a caulker in the shipyards. Members of the
railroad would assure him a warm welcome in that city.

He was free; Frederick Bailey was the name of a
slave. He decided he must have a new name to go with
his new life. So upon reaching New Bedford, Frederick
Bailey became Frederick Douglass.

Free! Frederick Douglass was soon to realize that his
color placed limitations on that freedom. He had no
difficulty finding a shipbuilder who was willing to hire
a caulker, but when he reported to work every white
man working at the shipyard threatened to leave the
job if he was allowed to stay. He had escaped his
slavemaster, but he could not escape race prejudice and
discrimination.

Only the most menial jobs were open to him. For
the next three years he worked as a day laborer. He
sawed wood, shoveled coal, swept chimneys, dug cel-
lars, loaded and unloaded ships. By hard work he was
able to support himself and his family. The family
grew. First a girl and then a boy were born.

A few months after moving to New Bedford, Douglass was given a copy of Garrison's *Liberator* and became a regular subscriber. "The paper became my meat and my drink," he wrote later. "My soul was set all on fire. Its sympathy for my brethren in bonds—its faithful exposures of slavery and its powerful attacks upon the upholders of the institution—sent a thrill of joy through my soul such as I had never felt before!"

He already had the spirit of the abolitionist movement. From the *Liberator* he learned the principles behind the movement and the steps being taken to further emancipation. The paper filled him with hope, and he began to attend all the antislavery meetings held in New Bedford. William Lloyd Garrison became his hero.

Members of Garrison's New England Anti-Slavery Society toured the Northern states speaking against slavery. One evening in August, 1841, Douglass was attending one of these meetings when one of the abolitionists saw him in the crowd and invited him to speak. He was taken completely by surprise and trembled as he stood before the audience. Afterward he could not remember a single word he said, but the audience was impressed.

They saw a young man about twenty-four years old, six feet tall, with broad shoulders and a mass of black curly hair. His eyes were deep-set and steady, his lips were full, and his skin was bronze-colored. He spoke with a fine, strong voice, simply and from his heart.

In the audience that night was William Lloyd Garrison. He spoke after Douglass and, using the ex-slave as his example, gave the best speech of his career. At the end of the meeting he offered Douglass a job as a speaker for the Massachusetts abolitionists.

Frederick Douglass had found his life's work. All his natural talents—his clear and intelligent mind, his impressive physical appearance, his magnificent speaking voice—all these could be put to use in the cause that had for years been closest to his heart—the abolition of the slave system and the freedom of his people.

8

Liberty for All

The Massachusetts abolitionists, whom Douglass joined in 1841, were at the heart of the rapidly growing movement. Their leader, William Lloyd Garrison, had become the symbol of reform and rebellion throughout the country. In the whole of American history few white men have been so dedicated to black freedom as the young editor of the *Liberator*. Carrying the battle into the enemy camp, he staged sit-ins and freedom rides, traveling hundreds of miles, organizing and agitating. Dedicated to the principle of nonviolence, Garrison was mild in manner and soft in voice, yet he was driven by a passion for justice that knew no limits.

He was so devoted to the cause of the slave that many people who had not met him believed he was black. Garrison did not mind. "I never rise to address a colored audience," he said, "without feeling ashamed of my own color."

Closely associated with Garrison in his work was the young and elegant Wendell Phillips. Where Garrison excelled as the editor of his paper, Phillips shone as a great orator. He pleaded the cause of abolition so well that he could dominate the most hostile crowds.

It was with men like these that Frederick Douglass took his place, and within a short time he revealed himself as their equal. Others spoke well, but they did not have the firsthand knowledge that Douglass possessed. Drawing from his own years as a slave, he was able to make his audiences actually *live* slavery. William Wells Brown, himself a black abolitionist, said of him, "White men and black men had talked against slavery, but none had ever spoken like Frederick Douglass."

Enemies of abolition did all they could to stop the black man from speaking in their towns. As he traveled through the North, he was often greeted with boos and rotten eggs. Once an angry mob threw him down a flight of stairs; once he was beaten; another time his right hand was broken in a fight. But Douglass seemed to welcome danger. He sometimes walked through the streets of a town before his lecture ringing a bell to announce his presence and urging everyone to attend. Sometimes it was impossible to find a hall where meetings could be held. Even this did not stop Frederick Douglass. In one Northern city he simply took his stand under a large tree and began addressing a group of five people. Before long his audience had grown to 500. And always, as he spoke the people who heard him got a new view of the slavery issue. His sincerity and eloquence, as well as the argument of his own magnificent manhood, won many hearts to the cause of abolition.

As the movement gained in strength, slaveowners became more determined to keep and to regain their "property." Early in 1842 a Southerner appeared in Boston searching for his slave who had run away several years before. The black man, George Latimer, appealed to his abolitionist friends, and Frederick Douglass helped to raise funds so that Latimer could buy his freedom from his angry master. The case caused so much attention that the Massachusetts state government was forced to take a stand. It forbade its own state officers to help in the hunting down of fugitive slaves. For the time being, at least, the Northern states were still "free."

Yet in the Northern states the black men met with serious problems of discrimination and prejudice. Freedom from slavery did not mean freedom of opportunity. Like their brothers in slavery, the free blacks knew that only by uniting could they hope to fight for their rights as Americans. Beginning in 1831, Negro conventions were held each year. Free blacks from all over the country met in different Northern cities to discuss means of asserting their rights and improving the conditions of their lives.

As Frederick Douglass emerged as the young leader of his race, he began to take an active part in these conventions. There he met all the leading blacks of the time. J. W. C. Pennington, the well-known preacher who had performed his marriage ceremony, was a prominent member. So was J. McCune Smith, a physician with three degrees from the University of Glasgow in Scotland. Carpenters, shoemakers, tailors, engineers, merchants, painters, farmers, barbers and grocers—all were there. The black abolitionist leaders attended: Theodore S. Wright, William Jones, Charles Lenox Remond,

William Wells Brown, Samuel Ringgold Ward, and Henry Highland Garnet.

Samuel Ringgold Ward, "so black that when he closed his eyes you could not see him," was a powerful speaker. So was the twenty-seven-year-old Henry Highland Garnet. At the 1843 convention he called for a general slave strike. "Brethren, arise, arise!" he said. "Strike for your lives and liberty. Rather die freemen than live to be slaves. Remember you are four million. Let your motto be resistance! resistance! resistance!"

Douglass, who still hoped that abolition could be gained by peaceful means, was opposed to Garnet and his views. Although the two served the same cause for many years, they were never friends.

In fact, the conventions never achieved very much because of the differences in opinion among the members. Some of the black leaders favored colonization as a solution to the discrimination against their race. Douglass was one of those who opposed the plan. He called colonization "the twin sister of slavery."

At the Negro conventions and the abolitionist meetings the rights of black men were freely discussed. Yet in the halls of Congress, the gag rule still prevented any petition relating to the subject of slavery from being introduced. Only one man spoke out against this injustice, and finally, after eight years of fighting, John Quincy Adams won his battle. In 1844 the gag rule was repealed. A few years before Adams had once more proved himself to be the champion of freedom. This was in the *Amistad* affair.

The *Amistad* was a Spanish slave ship. One day in 1839 it set sail for a Cuban port with a cargo of fifty-three slaves. Among these was a young African named Cinqué, who had no intention of being sold as a slave. He led his fellow blacks in an uprising, killed the captain and most of the crew, and took control of the ship. However, since none of the blacks knew anything about navigation, they had to rely on the remaining crew members to guide the ship. These men changed the course of the ship until it arrived at New Haven, Connecticut. There Cinqué and his followers were arrested and put into jail.

Soon the handsome Cinqué had become the center of an international legal battle. Spain wanted the blacks to be tried for piracy; Southerners wanted them tried for murder. But John Quincy Adams volunteered his services as their lawyer. In his case before the Supreme Court, the old man argued that the slave trade was illegal and opposed to the natural rights of man and that the blacks were justified in rebelling. He pleaded so well that the court, with a majority of Southern judges, decided in his favor. Cinqué and his fellow blacks were freed and returned to Africa.

Yet Cinqué and George Latimer were exceptions to the rule. Even in the North, a runaway slave was no longer safe from his Southern master. Douglass came to realize this in 1845.

That year, when he was twenty-seven years old, he published the first of three books. Entitled the *Narrative of the Life of Frederick Douglass,* it told the story of his life as a slave in moving terms and soon became a best seller. But the publicity that Douglass received from his book spelled danger for the young author. What if his master, Thomas Auld, should come to New Eng-

land looking for him? What if one of many slave catch-
ers who operated in the North should arrest him and
lead him back to slavery? Since he was constantly in
the public eye, he had no way to protect himself. His
friends advised him to leave the country for a while.

So, after providing for his wife and children, he
sailed to England. Many of the English had read his
book, and he was received there as a celebrity. He
traveled around speaking against slavery before great
crowds. Everywhere he made friends; always he was
treated with respect. He was accepted at all the hotels,
rode in the best trains, met the most famous people.
Never did he meet with prejudice because he was black.
It was a great contrast to the treatment he received in
America, where he was often told, "We don't allow
niggers here."

Although his new friends urged him to bring his
family to live in England, Douglass was eager to get
back home. "I prefer to go home, to go back to America,"
he said. "I glory in the conflict. I go back for the sake
of my brethren. I go back to suffer with them, to toil
with them, to endure insult with them, to speak for
them, to struggle with them for freedom. I go back
gladly."

When his English friends saw that he was determined
to leave, they decided that he must return to America
as a completely free man. They collected money and
bought his freedom from Thomas Auld so that no
white man would have a claim on him. They also gave
Douglass a large sum of money to be used to start a
newspaper of his own. Armed with this, he returned to
the scene of the battle.

During Douglass' visit to England the United States had entered into a war with Mexico. When Mexico gained her freedom from Spain in 1821 her territory included California, New Mexico, and Texas. Large numbers of Americans had already moved into this territory, and at first the Mexican government encouraged the immigration. But in 1829 the Mexican president abolished slavery and ordered the centralization of the government. The Texas slaveowners rebelled. They had no intention of freeing their slaves. Organizing a small army, they drove the Mexicans out of Texas and set up the Lone Star Republic.

A few year later Texas was annexed to the United States. Now it was the Mexican government's turn to protest. It has been claimed that the United States President, James K. Polk, baited Mexico into war over Texas in order to gain the rich lands of California. In any case, war between the two countries was declared in April, 1846.

Many prominent Americans were opposed to the war. Among these was Henry Thoreau, who voiced his protest in his famous *Civil Disobedience*, but the war continued for two years. Finally, in February, 1848, the Mexicans admitted defeat and signed a peace treaty ceding Texas, New Mexico, and California to the United States.

Frederick Douglass called the treaty not "peace" but "plunder." He said, "They have succeeded in robbing Mexico of her territory, but that the end has come to the wholesale murder of Mexico is truly a just cause for rejoicing."

As a result of the Mexican War, General Zachary

Taylor, who had commanded the United States troops, was elected President in 1848, and the question of slavery in the newly acquired territory loomed large in the public mind.

Douglass' decision to start a newspaper of his own did not meet with the approval of William Lloyd Garrison. He felt that the black man could serve the cause of freedom best as a speaker. Although Douglass was grateful to Garrison for all he had done for him and his people, he longed to be independent.

Among the abolitionist groups two schools of thought were forming. Both worked for the emancipation of the slaves but differed as to the methods to be used. One group, headed by William Lloyd Garrison, was for revolution; the other group was for reform.

Garrison felt that the Constitution of the United States was a proslavery document in spirit as well as in fact, and he favored secession of the free states. "No union with slaveholders" was his motto. He saw nothing to be gained by political means. Nothing short of revolution could satisfy him.

Frederick Douglass sided with the political abolitionists who wanted to work within the framework of the existing government. They hoped that through the political power of the vote emancipation could be brought about.

When Douglass proposed starting his own newspaper, the differences between him and Garrison were brought to a head. The two men parted company. Douglass moved his family to Rochester, New York, where the political abolitionists under Gerrit Smith were already well established.

The first issue of the newspaper appeared in December, 1848. Douglass called it the *North Star* and explained his policy in an editorial. "We solemnly dedicate the 'North Star' to the cause of our long oppressed and plundered fellow countrymen. It shall fearlessly assert your rights, faithfully proclaim your wrongs and earnestly demand for you instant and even-handed justice. While it shall boldly advocate emancipation for our enslaved brethren, it will omit no opportunity to gain for the nominally free complete and equal rights."

Thus Douglass announced the two great goals of his life: freedom for the slaves and equal rights for the free blacks. He never ceased to speak out against the injustices tolerated in the "free" states of the North.

His daughter Rosetta, oldest of his five children, attended a private school in Rochester, but because she was black she was put in a classroom by herself. Douglass wrote a long letter to the Rochester papers protesting this action. He took his daughter out of the school and organized a movement against segregation. With characteristic zeal he kept up the fight until the public schools in Rochester were desegregated.

In his speeches he constantly condemned prejudice. He worked for economic opportunity for blacks and insisted that they should have the same rights as whites "in the churches and schools, in the armed forces, at the voting box, on juries."

When he traveled he paid no attention to the WHITE ONLY signs. If he was told to go to the Jim Crow car, he refused. Once on an Eastern railroad he went to the very best car. When the conductor came along and ordered him to leave he asked why. On being told it was because he was black, he simply refused to move. Six men surrounded him and said if he didn't move, they would drag him out. He just sat there. They grabbed his head and shoulders, but he was prepared. He wrapped his legs around the seat, and when the men dragged him out they tore the whole seat up with him!

Frederick Douglass was a true reformer. While he never missed a chance to fight for his black brothers, he worked for other reforms as well. He was one of the generation of which Ralph Waldo Emerson wrote, "Young men were born with knives in their brains." Like Emerson, he tried to get Americans to free their minds of hatred and prejudice and think out the consequences of democracy.

Douglass was a pioneer in the movement for women's rights. The women of his day had no rights before the law; they could not make contracts, testify in court, or vote. Such injustice moved the black reformer, and he joined Elizabeth Stanton, Lucretia Mott, and other leaders of the movement in demanding equality. He was also active in the temperance movement and worked for the abolition of capital punishment.

One of his greatest friends and supporters was the white abolitionist Gerrit Smith, who had devoted his life to the cause of the black race. This generous man gave 140,000 acres of land in western New York State to 3,000 blacks. The gift was an important one since no one could vote in New York unless he owned real estate. By giving these black men land, Smith was also giving them the right to vote.

One year after Douglass and his family moved to

Rochester gold was discovered in California. People rushed to stake out a claim and get rich. The population of California grew so quickly that within two years the territory was applying for admission to the Union as a free state. Once more the balance of power between the free and slave states was threatened.

As antislavery forces grew, the South closed in on itself. Southern whites decided that slavery must be a permanent basis for American society. They marshaled their strength to preserve their way of life. Once again Northern politicians bowed to the slaveowners. In the Compromise of 1850 California was admitted as a free state, but a new federal Fugitive Slave Law was passed. This law made the federal government responsible for the return of any runaway slave and imposed severe penalties on anyone who helped or concealed a fugitive. The United States government became an instrument in the hands of the slaveowners.

A wave of protest swept through the North. Emerson called the law "this filthy enactment" and declared, "I will not obey it, by God!" Garrison was so enraged he burned a copy of the Constitution, shouting as he did, "So perish all compromise with tyranny." The response of the blacks was swift and militant. Speeches were made, petitions signed. Douglass condemned the law in a famous speech delivered in December, 1850. "The whole American people are responsible for slavery and must share in its guilt and shame," he declared.

Regardless of the new law, the Underground Railroad continued to operate. Frederick Douglass was active as one of its agents. Often when he went to his newspaper office, he would find a runaway slave hiding there. He fed the slaves, hid them until dark, and then sent them on their way to Canada. Much of the money he earned making speeches was used to help these fugitives.

Through this work he became a friend of Harriet Tubman's, a renowned black conductor on the railroad. When only nineteen years old, this remarkable woman set out alone from her Maryland home and somehow managed to reach Philadelphia. That was in 1849. A year later she was back in the South again, leading her sisters and children to freedom. In all she returned to the South nineteen times, conducting more than 300 slaves throught the North to safety in Canada.

Although she could not read or write, she had a natural talent as an actress. When threatened with capture she would quickly turn herself into a feeble old woman. However, she always carried a pistol at her side in case this act did not work. Rewards up to $12,-000 were posted for her capture.

Douglass was deeply impressed by Harriet's work. He wrote to her, "Most of what I have done has been public. You have labored in a private way. I have the applause of the crowd while the most that you have done has been witnessed by a few trembling, scared and footsore bondsmen. The midnight sky and the silent stars have been the witnesses of your devotion and your heroism."

Yet Douglass knew that escape to Canada could never be the solution for America's millions of slaves. As the political abolitionists organized for action, he became a leader in the Liberal Party. For several years this party had backed James G. Birney for President of the United

States. As the first antislavery candidate, Birney won
only about two percent of the votes, but the campaign
helped to bring the issue of slavery before the public.
The party hoped for greater success in the future.

In 1851 the *North Star* became the official newspaper
of the party and its name was changed to *Frederick
Douglass' Paper*. The black man also used his great
gifts as a public speaker in campaigning for the party's
candidates, and in 1852 his friend Gerrit Smith was
elected to the United States Congress.

Smith was in Congress in 1854, when the Kansas-
Nebraska Bill came before the House. Once again the
slavery issue dominated the poltical scene. By the terms
of the Missouri Compromise of 1820, the territory of
Nebraska had been closed to slavery forever, but the
new bill repealed the former law. It divided the territory into two parts, Kansas and Nebraska, and provided
that the question of slavery should be decided by the
inhabitants of the area. This was a victory for the proslavery cause. Smith, who had opposed the bill with
all his might, resigned his seat in protest.

The new law brought action from another of Frederick Douglass' friends, the fiery white man John Brown.
He was working for the Underground Railroad in Missouri when the law was passed and immediately went
into Kansas to combat the proslavery forces in that
territory.

Brown had been working in the cause of freedom for
many years before 1848, when he first met Douglass.
The two men became friends immediately, and Brown
regarded the black man as a kindred spirit. Both were

fighters, both fought for the same cause, yet the means they adopted were quite different.

The Kansas-Nebraska Bill produced another kind of action. A new political party was organized. Known as the Republicans, the new group was opposed to the extension of slavery. It nominated John C. Frémont for President in 1856 and conducted a lively campaign calling for "free soil, free speech and Frémont."

Douglass was critical of the Republicans. "They do not give a full recognition to the humanity of the Negro," he said. The Republicans were not interested in freeing the slaves but simply in limiting slavery to the states that already had it. Douglass knew this was not enough. "Liberty must cut the throat of slavery or have its own throat cut by slavery," he claimed. In the 1856 election he and his abolitionist friends formed themselves into a new Radical Abolitionist Party.

It was a Democrat, James Buchanan, who took office as President in March, 1857, just two days before the Supreme Court made its famous Dred Scott Decision.

Dred Scott was a slave who had been taken by his master from Missouri first to the free state of Illinois, then to a territory where slavery was prohibited, then back again to Missouri. Scott sued his master for his freedom on the grounds that he had been a citizen of free territory twice. The Supreme Court decided against Scott on three counts. It claimed that as a black he could not be a citizen of the United States and had no right to sue in a federal court and that as a resident of Missouri the Illinois laws no longer affected him. Furthermore, the Southern judges went on to declare that the Missouri Compromise was unconstitutional and that "slavery followed the flag." In effect, the court declared that slavery was national and freedom was sectional.

No measure angered the abolitionists and the black population as much as the Dred Scott Decision. Douglass, speaking on the subject before an abolitionist meeting, saw one cheerful sign. He said, "This very attempt to blot out forever the hopes of an enslaved people may be one necessary link in the chain of events leading to the complete overthrow of the whole slave system." He proved to be a prophet.

Douglass' breadth of vision was not shared by his friend John Brown. Impatient over the slow progress of the abolitionists, Brown decided to take personal action against the slave system. He knew that among the slaves there were many who would rally to his aid at the first opportunity, and he began to work out a plan.

In the town of Harpers Ferry, Virginia, was a large government arsenal. Brown planned to lead a surprise attack against the town, take over the arsenal, and use it as a base for a general slave revolt.

For several months he traveled through the North, raising money and recruiting men. He was a frequent guest at the Douglass home in Rochester and asked his friend to join him in the raid. "Come with me, Douglass," he said. "I will defend you with my life. I want you for a special purpose."

But Frederick Douglass could not approve of Brown's plan of action. Long ago he had made his choice of weapons. He fought with words, not guns.

On October 16, 1859, Brown and his small band of thirteen whites and five blacks attacked the arsenal at

Harpers Ferry. They killed the mayor of the town and took some of the people prisoners. Immediately state and federal troops were sent out to fight them. A bloody skirmish followed. Brown's men were far outnumbered, but they fought with remarkable courage. One of their prisoners wrote later, "Brown was the coolest and firmest man I ever saw in defying danger and death." With his two sons dead at his side, the valiant champion of human rights went right on fighting until marines finally captured him. There were only five men left to be taken prisoners. All were hanged for murder a few weeks later.

Of Brown's five black companions, two were killed in the fighting. They were Lewis Sheridan Leary and Dangerfield Newby. Two others were captured with Brown. One, Shields Green, had been introduced to Brown by Frederick Douglass. The other, Anthony Copeland, Jr., was a graduate of Oberlin College. He wrote to his parents from his prison cell: "My fate is sealed but let this not occasion you any misery. Remember the cause in which I was engaged; remember that it was a Holy Cause."

Copeland and Green were hanged. The fifth black, Osborn Anderson, managed to escape and live to fight for freedom again in the Civil War.

At his trial John Brown said, "I pity the poor in bondage who have none to help them. That is why I am here. It is my sympathy with the oppressed and wronged who are as good as you and as precious in the sight of God. If it is necessary that I lose my life in the cause of justice, I say, let it be done."

Brown's heroic death won him fame throughout the

North. Soon the song "John Brown's Body" was being sung everywhere in the North.

Frederick Douglass was known to be a good friend of the martyr Brown, and the federal government, thinking that he had taken part in the plot, issued a warrant for his arrest. Douglass fled to Canada. There he wrote an explanation of his actions which was published in the Rochester papers. He said that he had no part in the plan. He pointed out that each man must choose his own means of fighting the evil of slavery and his means were different from Brown's. Later he paid tribute to his old friend, saying, "If John Brown did not end the war that ended slavery, he did at least begin the war that ended slavery. Until this blow was struck, the prospect of freedom was dim. When John Brown stretched forth his hand the time of compromise was gone."

From Canada Douglass went to England, where he was received by his friends. His family remained behind in their comfortable brick house in Rochester, New York. Rosetta, Lewis, Frederick, Jr., and Charles were all teen-agers, and their famous father was very proud of them. But his youngest child, ten-year-old Annie, was his favorite. "The light and life of my house," he called her. During the weeks her father was abroad Annie became sick and died. It was a great sorrow to Douglass who hurried home to be with his grief-stricken family.

The 1860 Presidential campaign was approaching, and Douglass threw himself into his work vigorously. The Republicans had gained control of Congress in the elections of 1858 and had a good chance of winning in 1860. They chose as their candidate Abraham Lincoln, whose humble birth, homely wit, and skill in debate could be counted on to win many votes in the North. In 1858 he had declared, "A house divided against itself cannot stand. I believe this government cannot endure permanently half slave and half free."

Yet the Republican Party had no place in it for abolitionists. It took its stand against the extension of slavery into the territories but had no intention of interfering with slavery in the Southern states.

Frederick Douglass hoped that Abraham Lincoln would win the election. He realized that the party did not go far enough on the question of slavery, but it offered a chance to do some good—and it had a chance of winning. During the campaign he wrote, "The slaveholders know the day of their power is over when a Republican President is elected."

In November of that year Abraham Lincoln was elected President.

For the Southern states this was the last straw. One month after the election South Carolina seceded from the Union. Mississippi, Alabama, Florida, and Georgia soon followed. In February, 1861, Louisiana and Texas joined the seceded states and the Confederacy was founded.

The reasons for secession were set forth clearly. "The people of the Northern states have enticed our slaves from us. . . . They claim the right to exclude slavery from the territories. . . . They have denounced as sinful the institution of slavery; they have permitted the open establishment among them of abolition societies and have united in the election of a man to the high office of President of the United States whose opinions and purposes are hostile to slavery."

"State's rights" were also claimed as a cause of the break, but, in fact, the South criticized the Northern states for trying to use the principle of state's rights to protect themselves against the Fugitive Slave Law and the Dred Scott Decision.

By the time Lincoln was inaugurated on March 4, 1861, all the forts and Navy yards in the South had fallen into Confederate hands except two. One of these was Fort Sumter near Charleston, South Carolina, where a small Union force refused to join the Confederates. The commander of the fort asked the United States government to send reinforcements, but before they arrived, on the morning of April 12, 1861, Confederate guns fired on Fort Sumter, and the war between the states began. On hearing the news, Frederick Douglass exclaimed, "God be praised!"

Douglass saw the war as a crusade for freedom. For him it was a war for humanity and its purpose was to crush the slave system.

Lincoln's view was quite different. His main concern was to preserve the Union. With the firing on Fort Sumter, Virginia seceded and joined the Confederacy; Arkansas, Tennessee, and North Carolina followed shortly after. But five border states were still undecided. The western counties of Virginia, later to become West Virginia, remained in the Union. So did Missouri, Kentucky, Delaware, and Maryland. These were slave states. If Lincoln was to take a firm stand against slavery, he might drive these border states out of the Union. Black emancipation was to be an outgrowth rather than the object of the war.

Lincoln's first act after the fall of Fort Sumter was

to call for 75,000 volunteers to fight for the Union. Blacks in the North responded eagerly. Everywhere meetings were called and groups of volunteers began drilling. But when blacks reported for enlistment, they were refused. They were told that this was a "white man's war."

Douglass was furious. Writing in his newspaper, he expressed his views: "Let the slaves and free colored people be called into service and formed into a liberating army to march into the South and raise the banner of Emancipation among the slaves." His plea went unheeded, for the Lincoln administration feared large black forces would antagonize the wavering border states.

It was a "whites only" army that marched into Virginia in July, 1861, confident that the whole thing would be over in ninety days. They were headed for Richmond, the Confederate capital, but after a hard day of fighting at the Battle of Bull Run, the same men straggled back to Washington in defeat. There was no more talk of a ninety-day war.

The Union strategy was formed. In the East, the Army of the Potomac would push South again to capture Richmond, while the Army in the West gained control of the Mississippi River. The Navy would support the Army by attacks on the coastal cities, a blockade of Southern ports, and a patrol of the Western rivers.

To the four million slaves of the South, the Union forces were indeed a liberating army. Although there were many instances of individual loyalty to white masters, the magic word of freedom was whispered in every quarter. Keeping themselves well informed on events of the war, they adopted a policy of watchful waiting.

Their chance came in May, 1861, when three slaves from Virginia took refuge in the Army camp of General Benjamin Butler. When their owner demanded their return, Butler refused, claiming that the black men were "contraband" of war. This declaration triggered a massive flight of blacks to the Union lines. Everywhere Union camps were overrun with fugitive slaves, most of them eager to fight. They were put to work felling trees, digging trenches, cooking, and driving wagons.

There was no stopping the blacks when the Yankees were around. Southern patrols were increased, but without success. The fugitive slaves brought to the Union camps an eagerness to serve, a disregard for danger, and a knowledge of the South that was invaluable to the invading troops. "Whenever a Negro appeared with a shovel in his hand," one man wrote, "a white soldier took his gun and returned to the ranks."

Congress permitted the Army generals to make use of the fugitive slaves, but it made it clear that the war was being waged to maintain the Constitution and preserve the Union—not to interfere with slavery. However, some of the generals took another view of the matter.

In the West, John C. Frémont declared martial law in Missouri, stating that all Confederate property was confiscated and all slaves were freed. This action was received enthusiastically by the abolitionists, but Lincoln ordered the proclamation to be changed to include only those slaves who had been used by the Southerners for military purposes.

Farther south, the war had turned Major General

David Hunter into an abolitionist. In May, 1862, he issued a proclamation freeing all the slaves in the Department of the South, which he commanded. He sent out a call for fugitives to join the Army and started drilling them for action. Lincoln reversed the order, but the stampede of blacks to the Union side was not to be stopped. Young and old, sick or healthy, they were on the move toward freedom.

The Union Army was faced with a new problem. Black refugees must be fed, clothed, and housed. As their numbers increased, crowded conditions brought on disease, and medical attention was needed. Able-bodied blacks, both men and women, could be put to good use, but who would care for the old, the sick, and the children?

The abolitionists organized themselves into freedom relief societies. Clothes, bedding, sewing materials, garden seeds, farm implements, and medicines were purchased and sent South. Henry Highland Garnet and Frederick Douglass were active in organizing this work and collecting the necessary funds. Teachers left their Northern homes to set up schools in the "contraband" camps. Notable among these teachers was a young black woman from Philadelphia, Charlotte Forten, who sailed from New York to Sea Islands, South Carolina, to assist the freedmen.

Gradually the Union was becoming aware of the implications of slavery. Men asked themselves what was the good of restoring the Union if slavery, the cause of the break, was allowed to continue?

Lincoln finally said, "The moment came when I felt that slavery must die that the nation might live."

Like some before him in the Presidency, Lincoln wondered if the solution to the problem of black Americans lay in immigration to a country of their own. As his decision to free the slaves took form, he investigated plans to relocate freedmen in Haiti or Liberia.

Yet the fortunes of war were uppermost in everyone's mind. The Army of the Potomac under General George B. McClellan engaged General Robert E. Lee's forces in Virginia and met with repeated defeats. Lee's troops were driven back from Union territory.

Five days after Lee's defeat at the Battle of Antietam in Maryland, Lincoln declared that on January 1, 1863, he would issue a proclamation freeing all the slaves within the rebel states. In doing so, he gave the Confederacy 100 days to review its position. If no offer of peace was made by that time, the United States would proclaim their slaves to be "then, thenceforward, and forever free."

Meanwhile, the Union troops were counting their losses and looking for additional manpower. On August 14, General Ben Butler informed the Secretary of War that his forces at New Orleans were threatened by attack. "I shall call on Africa to intervene," he stated, "and I do not think I shall call in vain." Butler issued an order authorizing the enlistment of free Negroes, and the First Regiment of Louisiana Native Guards was formed. Butler acted without authority, but a few weeks later the War Department authorized limited enlistment of blacks in South Carolina and Kansas.

Colonel Thomas Wentworth Higginson resigned his command with a Massachusetts regiment to become the white commander of the First South Carolina Volunteers. Recruited largely from Hunter's disbanded troops, the Volunteers soon saw action at St. Simons Island off Georgia. There an ex-slave named John Brown became perhaps the first black man to fall under arms in the war.

Higginson was justly proud of his men as they paraded before him—"a regiment of freed slaves marching on into the future," he said.

By November, 1862, the First Kansas Volunteers, an all-black regiment, had seen action at Island Mounds, Missouri, and another regiment of ex-slaves was being enlisted in Tennessee.

For the abolitionists in the North the days dragged on toward the fateful first of January. Would Lincoln keep his promise? Would he really free the slaves? By that time the blacks knew Lincoln. He was a good man, kind and honest. But on the issue of slavery they believed he had proved himself slow, timid, changeable. Could he be trusted to carry out his latest policy of emancipation?

New Year's Day was known as Heartbreak Day throughout the South, for it was then that sales of slaves took place, separating parents from children and husbands from wives. Would New Year's Day, 1863, prove to be another heartbreak day to blacks and abolitionists in the North?

If some of the friends of slaves had their doubts, they still looked forward to the great day of promised freedom and made plans for celebrating the event.

The first day of the New Year came. Frederick Douglass and his friends gathered at Tremont Temple in Boston. William Wells Brown, William Lloyd Garrison, Harriet Beecher Stowe, and Charles B. Ray were all there, together with a large crowd of black and white Americans who had given much of their lives to the abolitionist cause.

No word had come from Washington, and they did not know whether the proclamation was signed or not. Hopefully, they spent the afternoon and evening listening to speeches. Douglass spoke, hailing "the rosy dawning of the new truth of freedom." Time passed. Still no word came from Washington. Even Douglass began to doubt. Eight o'clock came. Nine o'clock. Ten o'clock. Still no word.

Finally, shortly after ten news arrived by telegraph. A messenger burst into Tremont Temple, shouting, "It's coming! It's on the wires!" Lincoln had signed the proclamation. The slaves were free.

Immediately everyone was on his feet, shouting, laughing, and weeping. Then Douglass' rich baritone voice broke into song and all joined in the chorus, "Blow ye the trumpet, blow." Midnight came but no one was in the mood for bed. They kept singing and thanking God until dawn.

Similar celebrations were held throughout the North. In Washington, D.C., nearly 600 blacks from a nearby "contraband camp" spent the last night of the old year in prayer and celebrated their new freedom with songs that could be heard a mile away. On Sea Islands, South Carolina, the First South Carolina Volunteers, made up of 800 newly freed slaves, assembled in a grove of oak trees near their camp. People came from all over to listen as the soldiers stood at attention and the Emancipation Proclamation was read. Then suddenly a single voice broke into song, and all the blacks joined in:

My country, 'tis of thee,
Sweet land of liberty,
Of thee I sing.

9

The Nation's Wounds

With the Emancipation Proclamation, the Civil War
became a fight against slavery. Even though military
necessity was given as the reason for the action, blacks
and abolitionists were enthusiastic in their approval. As
Frederick Douglass put it, they "saw in its spirit a life
and power beyond its letter." Others in the North were
equally as enthusiastic. A war to preserve the Union was
not a cause to stir every man's heart, but a war in the
name of freedom appealed to what was best and deepest in all.

Lincoln, realizing that the proclamation had won
the support of public opinion in Europe, declared it to
be the "central act of my administration and the greatest event of the nineteenth century."

Under the terms of the proclamation, freed slaves
were to be received into the Army, and within weeks the
Northern states had lifted their ban on black enlistment.
Douglass was jubilant. "Once let the black man get upon
his person the brass letters, U.S.; let him get an eagle
on his button and a musket on his shoulder," he de-

clared, "and there is no power on earth which can deny that he has earned the right to citizenship in the United States."

The work of the abolitionists was over, their victory won. They turned their attention toward restoring peace. The governor of Massachusetts, having received permission to raise two black regiments, asked Douglass to help him recruit men. It was the chance the black leader had been waiting for.

He printed a stirring call: "Men of Color, to Arms!" He wrote, "Liberty won only by the whites will lose half its luster. I urge you to fly to arms and smite with death the power that would bury the government and your liberty in the same hopeless grave."

He recruited 100 men for the Massachusetts Fifty-fourth Regiment. Too old to fight himself, he was proud to have two of his sons, Lewis and Charles, join the first group who went for training in Massachusetts.

By the end of May, 1863, the Fifty-fourth had finished its training and went to Boston to embark for South Carolina. Meanwhile, Rhode Island raised the first black artillery regiment.

Douglass traveled through New York and Pennsylvania recruiting more men. Connecticut, Michigan, Illinois, Indiana, Iowa,and Kansas also raised black units. When recruits ran out in the North, Congress permitted recruiting officers to go into the South to enlist more. In all, 186,000 black soldiers were enrolled in the Union Army.

In the Navy, where blacks had always been welcome, they accounted for one-fourth of all the sailors.

These black volunteers met with discrimination. They

received less pay for their services and had much less chance for advancement. No blacks were given commissions as officers. Furthermore, when a black man fell into the hands of the Southern enemy, he could expect no mercy.

Frederick Douglass would not rest until these injustices had been corrected. He asked for an interview with President Lincoln to plead the cause of his fellow blacks. The President greeted the former abolitionist warmly. He knew him well by reputation. Douglass presented the case of the black soldiers, requesting that they receive equal pay and promotion for merit, and he asked the government to insist that the Confederate Army give better treatment to captured blacks. Lincoln was sympathetic, but he claimed that the widespread prejudice against the black man made it impossible for him to move too fast on the Negro question. Douglass went away disappointed.

The Massachusetts Fifty-fourth Regiment took another form of action. Three times it was formed up for pay and each time refused to take the money; the men said they would rather serve without pay than endure the injustice of receiving less than that paid to white soldiers.

This action stirred the conscience of the nation, and a bill was passed in Congress providing for the same pay, uniforms, arms, equipment, rations, and medical service for all soldiers regardless of color. It was a great day for the men of the Fifty-fourth when they received back pay in full for their eighteen months of service.

In spite of the hardships of war, the morale of the black soldiers was high. They felt they were at last striking a fatal blow at slavery and had a personal stake in the war. They were proud to be soldiers. "They take to drill as a child takes to its mother's milk," one of their officers remarked. On the parade field, in the camp, or in battle, ex-slaves and free blacks were proving themselves in the Union Army.

In the spring of 1863 five black regiments from Louisiana were given the task of attacking Port Hudson on the lower Mississippi. This was the major obstacle to General Ulysses S. Grant's advance on the bastion of Vicksburg. As the men charged toward the fort, they ran into a storm of enemy fire. Falling back, they regrouped and attacked again. Once more they were driven back as their comrades fell dead around them. After six or seven charges, they were forced to give up. "They were exposed to a terrible fire and were dreadfully slaughtered," one witness reported; "all who witnessed these charges agree that their conduct was such as would honor any soldier."

Blacks proved themselves again at Milliken's Bend, Louisiana, where a Confederate force of 3,000 attacked their camp. The white army swarmed over the camp's fortifications and engaged the blacks in hand-to-hand battle. In the fierce struggle that followed the blacks behaved so bravely that their conduct was praised by the Secretary of War.

A few days after Vicksburg fell to Grant's forces, Port Hudson was captured and the Union controlled the whole Mississippi waterway.

Soon after, on July 18, 1863, the Massachusetts Fifty-fourth was preparing to attack Fort Wagner on Morris Island, South Carolina. The Union must take the fort if its attack against Charleston were to succeed, but the enemy position was well fortified. Captain Robert Gould Shaw, a young white officer in the Fifty-fourth, was proud of the fact his company had been chosen to lead the attack. So were Lewis and Charles Douglass, who were in his company. But as the black soldiers approached the fort, the enemy opened up with such a barrage of fire that the advancing line staggered. Many fell dead; others rushed forward to charge the barricade. Standing on the parapet, Shaw shouted to his men, "Rally! Rally!" A few moment later, he was shot through the heart and fell dead into the fort.

"I had my sword-sheath blown away while on the parapet of the fort," wrote Lewis Douglass to his father. "Swept down like chaff, still our men went on and on."

As a dozen blacks fell with Shaw, Sergeant William H. Carney grabbed the flag and ran to the head of the column. He planted the flag on the parapet and stayed there, flattened against the wall for half an hour. But the desperate struggle could not be kept up. Supporting troops did not move up fast enough, and the black regiment was forced to fall back. The surviving soldiers limped back to the Union line with the half-dead Carney among them.

Fort Wagner remained in enemy hands. More than 300 Union soldiers were buried there in a common grave. Among them was Captain Shaw.

As 1863 drew to a close, Union forces held Kentucky, Tennessee, a large part of Louisiana, Mississippi, and Florida and had complete control of the Mississippi River. Increasingly freed slaves saw action against their

former masters. Yet black men were not the only ex-
slaves to see action. Harriet Tubman, the famous agent
of the Underground Railroad, made yet another trip
to the South to nurse the wounded in the poorly staffed
Army hospitals. For two years she nursed the bedridden,
white and black alike, and was commended for her
"kindness and attention to the sick and suffering."

Mrs. Tubman operated as a scout too, moving freely
into enemy territory with a bandanna around her head,
noting military defenses and the positions of supplies
and ammunition. Another black woman who served the
Union forces was Susie King Taylor, who worked under
Clara Barton nursing the wounded.

In December, 1863, a meeting of the American Abolitionist Society was held in Philadelphia. With the freeing of the slaves, their work was over and they met to
rejoice over their victory. Frederick Douglass was in the
audience and at the demand of the crowd he took the
speaker's stand. Never more brilliant, the great orator
told the society that its work was not done. The freeing
of the slaves was simply the first step—now the reformers
must work for their advancement. Douglass claimed that
the best way to advance the black man's interest was to
help him win the right to vote. If the black man knew
enough to risk his life for his flag, he argued, he knew
enough to vote. He went on to claim that blacks should
sit in Congress at Washington. "You may as well make
up your minds that you have got to see something dark
down that way," he stated.

Many of the abolitionists did not agree with Douglass,
but, as usual, he echoed the views of America's blacks.
Already, in New Orleans, blacks had petitioned the

President and the Congress for the right to vote. The Civil War dragged on, but men everywhere looked to the future.

Abraham Lincoln worried about what would become of those blacks still behind enemy lines if the North were forced to grant peace terms to the Confederacy. He called on Frederick Douglass to come and talk over the problem with him. The meeting took place in August, 1864, and the two men discussed a plan for helping the blacks escape before peace came.

As it turned out, no such plan was needed. In March, 1864, General Grant was made commander in chief of all the Union forces and went east to operate against Lee and his troops, taking with him 20,000 black soldiers. General William Tecumseh Sherman started on his famous "march to the sea" across Georgia, and it was apparent that the surrender of the rebels was only a matter of time.

Victory on the battlefield greatly improved Lincoln's chances for reelection in November, 1864. Douglass gave him his support. Later he offered an interesting view of Lincoln: "He was a white man's President, entirely devoted to the welfare of white men. Though the Union was more to him than our freedom or our future, under his wise and beneficent rule we saw ourselves gradually lifted from the depths of slavery to the heights of liberty and manhood. Viewed from the genuine abolition ground, Abraham Lincoln seemed tardy, cold, dull and indifferent; but measuring him by the sentiment of the country which he was bound as a statesman to consult, he was swift, zealous, radical and determined."

The reelection of Lincoln, the pinch of the North's

blockade of its ports, Sherman's march to the sea, and Grant's constant hammering at Lee's defenses took the heart out of the South. When Lincoln was inaugurated for a second term on March 4, 1865, the Confederacy was sinking fast.

After the inauguration, a reception was given at the White House, and Frederick Douglass was one of the 2,000 people who went to pay their respects. The White House guards, seeing the black man, attempted to put him out, but Douglass appealed directly to Lincoln. The President received him kindly and talked with him while the other guests waited in line. It was the last meeting of the two.

Meanwhile, Grant's army hammered at the outnumbered Confederate forces defending Richmond. Black troops were the first to enter the Confederate capital when it fell on April 3, 1865. Immediately Grant went in pursuit of Lee's troops, which were now completely surrounded. Knowing that his position was hopeless, Lee surrendered to Grant at Appomattox Court House on April 9.

On April 14, in Washington, President Lincoln was assassinated while attending a theater performance and his death shocked the world.

The hard task of trying to bind the nation's wounds fell to Vice-President Andrew Johnson, who succeeded Lincoln. Though the four million ex-slaves were penniless, they were rich in hope. In January, 1865, Congress had passed a law abolishing slavery forever and only state ratification was necessary before the Thirteenth Amendment became part of the Constitution.

With the war's end, the Radical Republicans in Congress wanted to keep the Confederates out of Congress long enough to pass laws to protect the Southern blacks and secure them their rights before the law. For six weeks President Johnson seemed ready to follow this policy. Then Johnson offered amnesty to all Confederates, and political control of the South was placed once more in the hands of the former slaveowners.

Frederick Douglass viewed the condition of the freedman with alarm. He "was free from the individual master but a slave of society," he said. "He had neither money, property, nor friends. He was free from the old plantation, but he had nothing but the dusty road under his feet. He was free from the old quarter that once gave him shelter, but a slave to the rains of summer and the frost of winter. He was turned loose, naked, hungry, and destitute to the open skies."

In the months that followed the end of the war thousands of former slaves died of starvation and disease.

Southern whites still looked on the blacks as an inferior race and were determined to "keep the Negro in his place," by law if possible, by force if necessary. One of the first acts of the postwar state governments was to pass "Black Codes," which left the freedman in very much the same position he had been as a slave.

Douglass realized that the black man's only hope lay in the federal government. In March, 1865, Congress had set up the Freedmen's Bureau under General Oliver O. Howard for the relief of Southern blacks. The bureau did a fine work. It set up more than 100 hospitals and distributed food to millions of people; by the end of the year it had organized hundreds of schools where 90,000 blacks were being educated.

The ex-slave needed this assistance badly, but just as badly he needed the right to determine his own life and future. He needed the right to vote. With his usual foresight, Frederick Douglass had been saying this for years. Now he began to travel throughout the North, using his name and gifts as a speaker to win the ballot for his fellow blacks.

Douglass was not the only black man speaking out for equal rights. All through the South mass meetings were held, petitions were sent to the President and the Congress demanding equal rights, the ballot, and land for the newly freed blacks.

Some people argued that the ex-slaves were not ready to be given the vote. To this Douglass replied, "As one learns to swim by swimming, the Negro must learn to vote by voting."

At the Negro Convention of 1866, a delegation of prominent black leaders was chosen to carry the appeal directly to the President. The five men chosen were William Whipper, George T. Downing, John Jones, Frederick Douglass, and his son Lewis. President Johnson met them coldly and refused to listen to their request.

On leaving the White House, Douglass said to his companions, "The President sends us to the people, and we will go to the people."

It was in the United States Congress that the black men found the friends they needed—Senator Charles

Sumner of Massachusetts and Representative Thaddeus Stevens of Pennsylvania. Stevens was already seventy-three years old when the Civil War ended, and he had spent his entire life as a champion of the free black and the fugitive slave. Now as the leader of the House of Representatives, he was in a position to continue his long fight for black equality. Sumner looked on the issue as a moral one. "I am in morals, not in politics," he often said.

The Radical Republicans in Congress, under the leadership of these two men, defied the President and passed the Reconstruction Act of 1867, ordering the Southern states to hold constitutional conventions with the black population participating fully in the elections. They sent federal troops into the South to see that the orders were carried out.

Stevens was not satisfied that the blacks should have equal rights under the law but wanted to guarantee economic equality as well. He proposed that the federal government should provide each freedman with "forty acres and a mule." The bill was defeated. With no land of their own, the blacks were forced to lease land from former owners. Many went back to work in the cotton and tobacco fields, living in shacks provided by their former masters and existing on credit.

Thanks to Stevens and Sumner, the year 1868 was revolutionary. Constitutional conventions met throughout the South. Although the blacks had a place in the conventions, they were generally in the minority. Yet they insisted on their rights—free schools, the vote, and full citizenship for all. Many black men had important roles to play. Oscar J. Dunn, an ex-slave, became lieutenant governor of Louisiana, and black men were elected to seats in many state legislatures.

In South Carolina blacks were in the majority when the new state legislature met. One reporter described the House of Representatives thus: "The Speaker is black, the clerk is black, the doorkeeper is black, the little pages are black, the chairman of Ways and Means is black, and the chaplain is coal black."

These men set about to solve the problems created by the war. Many fine laws were passed. Free schools were opened, railroads and bridges built.

In July, 1868, the Fourteenth Amendment bestowed full citizenship on all people born in the United States. Two hundred and fifty years had passed since the first black child was born on American soil. That soil had been nourished by the blood and toil and bones of millions of blacks. Now, at last, the black American became a citizen of his country.

In March, 1869, Andrew Johnson's stormy term of office came to an end after he had narrowly missed impeachment. He was succeeded in the Presidency by Ulysses S. Grant, hero of the Civil War.

Meanwhile, Frederick Douglass continued his fight for the black ballot, and finally in 1870 the Fifteenth Amendment was passed and ratified. At last the Constitution of the United States defined that no state could deny the right to vote on account of "race, color or previous condition of servitude." There was great rejoicing among the black people throughout the country.

Douglass felt that his place was in the nation's capital, where he could use his influence on Capitol Hill. His newspaper had been discontinued after the war, and there was nothing to tie him tc Rochester anymore. His wife, Anna, had never been happy there. A simple woman who never learned how to read, she did not share her husband's interests and was not comfortable with his learned friends. In Washington, D.C., there was a large black population where she could find her own friends. So in 1872 the family moved to Washington.

Farther south, Reconstruction proceeded. The economic life of that section had been shattered by the war. Transportation had collapsed. The Southern states were in serious trouble, both economically and politically. If these problems were to be solved, the cooperation of all citizens would be needed. New to politics, the Southern black men had been thrown suddenly into power under conditions that would have been too much even for the most experienced statesmen. Yet even in such trying times, the blacks proved themselves over and over again.

Three black men served as lieutenant governors—in South Carolina, Mississippi, and Louisiana. Another served as secretary of state in Mississippi. In South Carolina, a black judge sat on the State Supreme Court, and sixteen black men served in Congress, representing Mississippi, Georgia, North and South Carolina, Alabama, Florida, and Louisiana.

While the blacks had influence in all the Southern state governments, they did not control any of them. Even in South Carolina, where they were in the majority, they were willing to cooperate with white people. All they asked for was equal political rights and equality before the law.

This was more than Southern planters were willing to grant. The former slaveowners bitterly resented the blacks who showed political ability or did well in office. They were surprised that they could do it and angry that they were allowed to do it. Their opposition took both legal and illegal forms. The Democratic Party was revived to oppose the Republicans in state and national politics—and the Ku Klux Klan was organized.

Within a few years the Klan had established a reign of terror, outrage, and crime which "forms a record of wrong among the most hideous in the history of any modern state." Under pressure from the Klan, black participation in politics declined sharply. Where terror did not keep the black people from voting, tricks were used. Ballot boxes were stuffed with white votes. The place for voting was kept secret from the blacks. Sometimes armed men stood on the roads leading to the polls to make sure that no blacks could exercise their constitutional right to vote.

The Democratic newspapers of the South accused black officeholders of graft and corruption. It is true that there was a great deal of corruption during this period, but it was by no means limited to any group or section of the country. In fact, compared to the graft of the Tweed Ring in New York City and the Gas Ring in Philadelphia, the Southern Republicans looked like amateurs.

Yet stories of corruption lost the black politicians many friends throughout the country. As President Grant took office for a second term in 1873, the tide was turning. The country as a whole was becoming tired of the

"Southern question." Even the Radical Republicans had become disgusted with state governments that had to be "propped up by national soldiers."

In the Southern states white men were quitting the Republican Party to join the Democrats, and the blacks desperately needed the help of the whites who were now leaving them.

Still, in the Senate Charles Sumner went on fighting for equal rights. His Civil Rights Bill called for "full and equal accommodations in inns, public conveyances on land and water, theaters, and other places of public amusement." It guaranteed the rights of blacks to serve on juries and called for "public schools open to all without distinction of race or color." But, in March, 1874, Sumner died without seeing his bill passed. At his bedside was his great friend Frederick Douglass, who with George Downing and Sumner Wormley listened as the dying man said, "You must take care of the Civil Rights Bill—don't let it fail! Don't let it fail!"

It was a year before his Civil Rights Bill became law, and then no mention at all was made of public schools. In the House to vote on the bill was Robert Elliott, a black man from South Carolina. In his first speech before Congress, Elliott spoke with passion of the black man's share in American history. "I am what I am," he stated, "and I believe in my own nobility." P. B. S. Pinchback was there from Louisiana, a report of the times describing him as "young, charming, daring . . . the best dressed Southern man we have in Congress." In March, 1875, Blanche Kelso Bruce joined his black brothers in Washington as Senator from Mississippi. Born a slave, Bruce became a prominent Senate leader.

Such men were typical of the new South. For seven years a social and political revolution had been going on —a revolution based on the conviction that all men are equal. The Reconstruction governments had made some mistakes, but they were by far the most democratic the South had ever known.

Democracy was on the wane as the 1876 elections drew near and the Southern landowners organized for action. Grant, whose administration was notable for corruption, was leaving office. "Every Democrat must feel honor bound to control the vote of at least one Negro, by intimidation, purchase, keeping away or as each individual may determine how he may best accomplish it," Southern whites were told. "Never threaten a man individually. If he deserves to be threatened, the necessities of the times require that he should die."

While Democrats won in most of the Southern states, the Presidential election was so close that it hung in the balance for several weeks. In the end a political deal was made. Republican Rutherford B. Hayes would be given the necessary electoral votes to make him President, and in return the Southern Democrats would get "the right to control their affairs in their own way." Federal troops would be withdrawn from the South and the "Negro question" would be dropped.

In a matter of months the Fourteenth and Fifteenth amendments became dead letter laws all through the South, the Civil Rights Act was never enforced, and the Black Codes once more ruled the Southern black men.

In speech after speech Frederick Douglass denounced America for abandoning the black man. It was impossible, he said, to degrade the black people without degrading the social fabric of America. And he warned the American people: "Hungry men will eat. Desperate men will commit crime. Outraged men will seek revenge."

Though his words were not heeded, Douglass himself was esteemed by many Americans. In 1876 he was asked to speak at the unveiling of a monument to Abraham Lincoln, a monument given by black people who had raised more than $16,000. It showed Lincoln holding the Emancipation Proclamation in one hand, while his other hand was held over a slave. The slave was rising from the ground and the chains on his wrists were broken. Douglass didn't like this. He complained, "It shows the Negro on his knees. Freedom should be expressed by a more manly attitude."

In the audience that day were the President of the United States, his Cabinet, the Supreme Court Justices, and many Congressmen. Douglass was an impressive figure as he stood before them to deliver his speech. His hair and beard were white now, but he was erect and tall, and his eyes flashed as he spoke. His voice was as rich and full as ever. In an era of great orators, he was one of the greatest, and this occasion was the high point of his brilliant career.

Since the time of Lincoln Frederick Douglass had been a staunch Republican. He had worked hard for the party, and his great influence with the black people made him a key figure. His loyalty was rewarded in 1877 when President Hayes named him U. S. marshal of the District of Columbia. The appointment was an honor for a black, and Douglass willingly accepted. At the end of his term as marshal he led the procession through the Capitol for the inauguration ceremony of the new President, James A. Garfield. Garfield appointed Douglass recorder of deeds for the District of Columbia, a post he held for several years.

Even as a government official, Douglass never missed a chance to speak out against policies he felt unwise and practices that were prejudiced or unjust. His words carried weight, especially among the black people who looked to him for leadership.

He moved to a large house in Washington called Cedar Hill, where he was able to keep open house for his friends and relatives. All his children were married by this time, and he had many grandchildren who frequently visited him. Black people were always welcome at his home. He gave them advice, recommended them for jobs, and helped them out with loans and gifts of money. As America's best-known black and leader of his race, he continued to press the cause of his brothers.

In 1882 Anna Douglass died. Less than two years later Douglass shocked his black friends by marrying a white woman. Many were outspoken in their disapproval and accused Douglass of lacking race pride. His own children were so angry that they would not speak to his new wife.

To all this Douglass replied, "What business has any man to trouble himself about the color of another man's wife?"

The new Mrs. Douglass, the former Helen Pitts, came from a prominent white family and had worked as Douglass' secretary in the recorder's office. She said of her marriage, "Love came to me and I was not afraid to marry the man I loved because of his color."

There is no doubt that the marriage was a happy one. Douglass wrote to a friend saying that it had "brought strong criticism, but there was a peace and happiness within." Helen shared his interests. Together they traveled to Europe, visiting Douglass' old friends in England and touring the Continent.

The Republican Party was anxious to have Douglass home in time for the 1888 Presidential elections. He was its leading vote-getter among the blacks of the North. At the national convention he was assigned to cover four key states; although seventy years old, he worked day and night campaigning for Republican Benjamin Harrison.

After the election President Harrison rewarded Douglass by appointing him minister resident and consul general to the Republic of Haiti. Some blacks were not pleased. They said he could not be spared to go to Haiti when there was still so much to do for the advancement of the race at home in the United States. Douglass, used to criticism, accepted the appointment.

When he arrived in Haiti in October, 1889, Douglass personally was received warmly. But the Haitians were not receptive to his chief mission. The United States wanted to lease Môle-Saint-Nicolas as a naval base, and Douglass was assigned to carry out the negotiations. In this he failed when the Haitian government firmly turned down the proposal. After two years he resigned and returned to the United States.

In 1892 Grover Cleveland, a Democrat, was elected President. As a Republican, Douglass' life in public office was ended. He retired to private life at Cedar Hill and occupied himself with reading, corresponding, and preparing speeches.

To the end he was in demand as a public speaker. The day of his death, February 20, 1895, he was scheduled to speak at a Washington church. He died of a heart attack, quickly.

A few months before his death, a young black student, visiting Douglass, asked the old man what advice he would give to a young man who wanted to work for the advancement of his race. Frederick Douglass answered in words that summed up his own long and fruitful career: "Agitate. Agitate. Agitate."

In a time of crisis, three roads are open to a man—retreat, revolt, and reform. Douglass chose the most difficult of the three—reform. While he worked within the system, he never gave in to it. He never ceased to protest against injustice, agitate for reform, and work for the freedom of all mankind.

Index

189

190

191

The Author

RUTH WILSON teaches fifth grade in a public school in the central Harlem area of New York City. Born in Salt Lake City, Utah, she now leads a busy life in New York. She wrote *Our Blood and Tears*, her first book, while teaching full time and working for her master's degree at New York University.